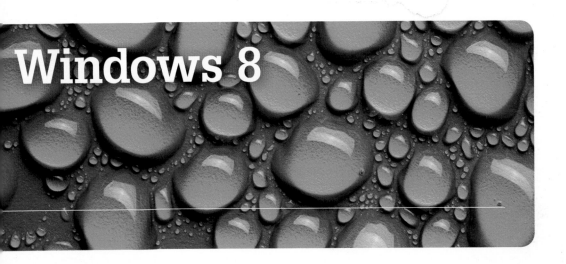

Windows 8

PEARSON

Harlow, England • London • New York • Boston • San Francisco • Toronto • Sydney • Auckland • Singapore • Hong Kong
Tokyo • Seoul • Taipei • New Delhi • Cape Town • São Paulo • Mexico City • Madrid • Amsterdam • Munich • Paris • Milan

Pearson Education Limited

Edinburgh Gate
Harlow CM20 2JE
Tel: +44 (0)1279 623623
Website: www.pearson.com/uk

First published 2013 (print and electronic)

Pearson Education is not responsible for the content of third-party internet sites.

ISBN: 978-0-273-78431-9 (print)
      978-0-273-78432-6 (PDF)

British Library Cataloguing-in-Publication Data
A catalogue record for the print edition is available from the British Library

Library of Congress Cataloging-in-Publication Data
A catalog record for the print edition is available from the Library of Congress

10 9 8 7 6 5 4 3 2 1
17 16 15 14 13

Cover image © Irina Tischenko/shutterstock

Print edition typeset in 11/14pt ITC Stone Sans by 3
Printed and bound in Great Britain by Scotprint, Haddington

NOTE THAT ANY PAGE CROSS-REFERENCES REFER TO THE PRINT EDITION

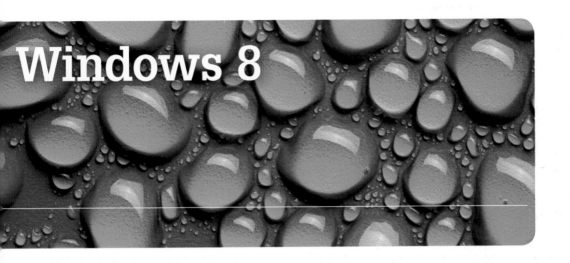

Windows 8

Simple
steps

Joli Ballew

Use your computer with confidence

Get to grips with practical computing tasks with minimal time, fuss and bother.

In *Simple Steps guides* guarantee immediate results. They tell you everything you need to know on a specific application; from the most essential tasks to master, to every activity you'll want to accomplish, through to solving the most common problems you'll encounter.

Helpful features

To build your confidence and help you to get the most out of your computer, practical hints, tips and shortcuts feature on every page:

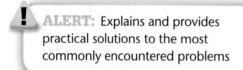 **ALERT:** Explains and provides practical solutions to the most commonly encountered problems

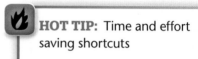 **HOT TIP:** Time and effort saving shortcuts

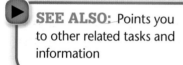 **SEE ALSO:** Points you to other related tasks and information

 **DID YOU KNOW?** Additional features to explore

WHAT DOES THIS MEAN?
Jargon and technical terms explained in plain English

Practical. Simple. Fast.

in **Simple** steps

Dedication:

For everyone in my life who supports me, helps me stay healthy, and enjoys my work.

Author's acknowledgements:

The older I get and the more books I write, the more people there are to thank and acknowledge. I am thankful for many things, including the opportunities offered by Pearson Education every time there's a new Windows edition, and the awesome team of editors and typesetters who work tirelessly to turn my words into pages and those pages into books.

I am thankful that I have a supportive family, including Jennifer, Andrew, Dad and Cosmo. I am thankful to my extended family for all playing a role in my daughter's upbringing and success. I am thankful for my health and sanity, much to the credit of my doctor, Kyle Molen. Between the lot of them, they keep me in check, on track, healthy and sometimes even sound.

I miss my mother, who passed away in February 2009, but I am thankful that some day I'll be able to see and talk to her again, something she worked hard to make me understand shortly after she passed away.

And finally, I'm thankful to my agent, Neil Salkind, who encourages me, is my biggest fan and always has my back, no matter what. Everyone should have someone like that in their lives.

Publisher's acknowledgements

We are grateful to the following for permission to reproduce copyright material:

Screenshot on page 164, Adobe product screenshot reprinted with permission from Adobe Systems Incorporated.

In some instances we have been unable to trace the owners of copyright material, and we would appreciate any information that would enable us to do so.

Contents at a glance

Top 10 Windows 8 Problems Solved

Contents

Top 10 Windows 8 Tips

1 Get to know Windows 8

2 Personalise Windows 8

3 Use the basic apps

4 Use Internet Explorer

5 Set up and use Mail

6 View, navigate and share photos

7 View, manage and listen to music and media

8 Stay in touch with others

9 Install hardware and software

10 Use Desktop applications

11 Work with files and folders

12 Use public and private networks

13 Secure Windows 8

14 Fix problems

Top 10 Windows 8 Problems Solved

Top 10 Windows 8 Tips

Tip 1: Create a log-in PIN

When you log in you have to type a password. This can become tiring after a while, especially if you don't have a physical keyboard. Even if you do have a keyboard, typing a password still takes time. You can change your log-in requirements so that you need only enter a numeric personal identification number (PIN) instead.

1 On the Start screen, type PIN. (If you don't have access to a physical keyboard, from the Settings charm, tap Keyboard.)

2 On the right side of the screen, click Settings.

3 Click Create a PIN.

4 Click Create a PIN.

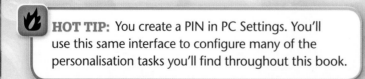

HOT TIP: You create a PIN in PC Settings. You'll use this same interface to configure many of the personalisation tasks you'll find throughout this book.

5 Type your current password, click OK, and then enter the desired PIN twice.

6 Click Finish.

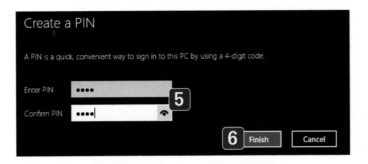

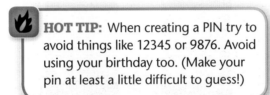

🔥 **HOT TIP:** When creating a PIN try to avoid things like 12345 or 9876. Avoid using your birthday too. (Make your pin at least a little difficult to guess!)

⚠ **ALERT:** Because we believe most of our readers will have a physical mouse (or the equivalent hardware on a laptop), we'll use the word *click* when we want you to click something with it. If you don't have a physical mouse, you'll need to tap the item instead. (Likewise, a double-click with a mouse is the same as a double-tap with your finger.)

Tip 2: Access the charms

Charms enable you to configure settings, share information, view devices, search for data and, as you know, access the Start screen. You can access the charms in many ways.

- Using touch, place your thumb in the middle of the right side of the screen and flick left (inwards).
- On a keyboard, use the key combination Windows key + C.
- On the screen, move the cursor to the bottom right corner, and when the transparent charms appear, move the cursor upwards.

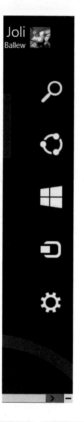

HOT TIP: If you're using a touch screen on a tablet, use your thumb to bring up the charms. On a touch screen monitor (such as one that might come with a desktop PC), try your right index finger instead.

DID YOU KNOW?
The Shut Down command is available from the Settings charm, from the Power icon that appears there.

Tip 3: Connect to a free wi-fi hotspot

Wi-Fi hotspots are popping up all over the country in cafés, parks, libraries and more. Wi-fi hotspots let you connect to the Internet without having to be tethered to an Ethernet cable or tied down with a high monthly wireless bill. These are public networks.

1 Get within range of the public wireless network.

2 Use the keyboard shortcut Windows key + I to access the Settings charm, then click the Network icon.

3 Click the desired network.

4 Place a tick in the Connect automatically box if you plan to connect to this network again, and then click Connect.

5 Click No, don't turn on sharing or connect to devices. This tells Windows you do not trust this network and want to consider it a public network (vs. a private one).

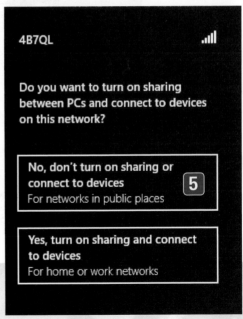

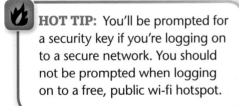

HOT TIP: You'll be prompted for a security key if you're logging on to a secure network. You should not be prompted when logging on to a free, public wi-fi hotspot.

ALERT: You'll need a laptop or tablet with the required wireless hardware to use a free wi-fi hotspot.

HOT TIP: To find a wi-fi hotspot close to you, go to http://maps.google.com and search for wi-fi hotspots.

Tip 4: Add tiles to or remove tiles from the Start screen

There are more windows, apps, programs and applications available than those that appear on the Start screen by default. There's the Calculator for instance, and Windows Media Player, Control Panel, Windows Explorer and Notepad, to name a few. You can add any item to the Start screen to have easier access to it. After you do, remove apps you won't use to further personalise the computer.

1 Right-click an empty area of the Start screen.

2 Click All apps.

3 Right-click an item you'd like to add.

4 From the bar that appears at the bottom of the page click Pin to Start. You can also choose Unpin from Start as applicable.

5 Return to the Start screen and locate the new tile. It will be placed on the far right.

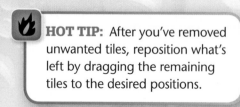

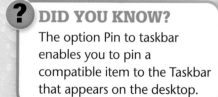

HOT TIP: After you've removed unwanted tiles, reposition what's left by dragging the remaining tiles to the desired positions.

? DID YOU KNOW?

The option Pin to taskbar enables you to pin a compatible item to the Taskbar that appears on the desktop.

6 Right-click or tap, hold and drag downwards on any tile you'd like to remove.

7 Repeat as desired to select additional tiles.

8 Click or tap Unpin from Start.

? DID YOU KNOW?

When you remove a tile from the Start screen you don't uninstall it. You can always access it (and even add it back) from the All apps screen.

Tip 5: Learn touch techniques

If your tablet does not have a physical keyboard, you'll rely on touch techniques to perform tasks, access data, type and so on. Although you'll learn more techniques as you work through this book, here are the more common ones.

1 Flick up from the bottom to access additional commands and features specific to the open app or window. Here's what you see when you flick upwards in Maps.

2 Flick from the middle of the left side of the screen inwards to move from one open app to another. When you do, one app slides in and the other slides out.

3 Flick from the middle of the right side of the screen inwards to access charms.

4 Tap any item to open it; tap and hold any item to select it; tap, hold and drag downwards a little to perform other tasks (such as to move an item).

5 Double-tap an item on the Desktop to open it.

6 Tap and hold an icon on the Desktop to access the contextual menu.

? **DID YOU KNOW?**

The tap-and-hold technique often produces what a traditional right-click does. A double-tap is like a double-click using a mouse. Likewise, tap-hold-and-drag is similar to holding down the mouse button and dragging an item.

Tip 6: Use File History

Most of the security features in Windows 8 are enabled by default. File History is not. File History saves copies of your files so you can get them back if they're lost or damaged. You'll need an external drive for File History for it to be effective.

1 Connect an external drive or make sure a network drive is available.

2 From the Start screen, type File History.

3 Click Settings, and then click File History.

4 In the File History window, click Turn on.

5 Wait while File History copies your files for the first time.

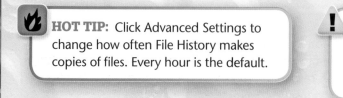

HOT TIP: Click Advanced Settings to change how often File History makes copies of files. Every hour is the default.

ALERT: If you ever need to restore files using File History, open the File History window and click Restore personal files.

Tip 7: Connect social accounts in the Photos app

You can view pictures stored on SkyDrive, Facebook or Flickr from the Photos app. These are all free, online storage spaces. You'll have to click their respective tiles and log in with your account first (if prompted) to use those areas though.

1 From the Photos app, on the landing page, click Facebook or Flickr.

2 Click Connect.

3 If prompted, type your email or user name, and your password.

HOT TIP: Once you connect you will be able to view the photos stored on your social networking sites from the Photos app.

❓ DID YOU KNOW?

If you decide later you don't want to connect to a specific social network, from Photos, from the Settings charm, click Options. From there you can disable any previously connected site. (Use the Windows key + C to access the default charms.)

Tip 8: Play a song

If you have music in your Music library you can play it from the Music app. If you don't have any music, you can copy songs from CDs you own.

1 Open the Music app and navigate to any song to play.

2 Click the song and click Play.

3 Repeat. As you add songs, click Add to Now Playing.

4 Explore the playback options at the bottom of the screen. You may have to flick up or right-click to access these.

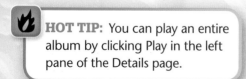

5 Click the album cover, located to the right of my music, to view the album cover, track list, artist information and more. (You can also click the thumbnail on the playback controls.)

HOT TIP: You can play an entire album by clicking Play in the left pane of the Details page.

? DID YOU KNOW?
As you add music to your Music library, the songs and albums will appear in the Music app automatically.

Tip 9: Use ReadyBoost to improve performance

ReadyBoost is a technology that enables you to use a USB flash drive or a secure digital memory card as cache (a place where data is stored temporarily and accessed when needed) to increase computer performance. Cache works like RAM, and more is certainly better!

1 Insert a USB flash drive, thumb drive or memory card into an available slot on the outside of your PC.

2 When prompted in the upper right corner, click to view your options.

3 Choose Speed up my system, Windows ReadyBoost.

4 Choose to dedicate the device to ReadyBoost and click OK.

> **! ALERT:** USB keys must be at least USB 2.0 and meet other requirements, but don't worry about that, you'll be told if the hardware isn't up to par.

> 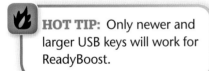 **HOT TIP:** Only newer and larger USB keys will work for ReadyBoost.

Removable Disk (F:)

Choose what to do with removable drives.

 Speed up my system
Windows ReadyBoost **3**

 Configure this drive for backup
File History

 Open folder to view files
Windows Explorer

 Take no action

WHAT DOES THIS MEAN?

RAM: Random access memory is where information is stored temporarily so the operating system has quick access to it. The more RAM you have, the better your PC should perform.

Cache: A temporary storage area similar to RAM.

Tip 10: Share data with Public folders

If you want to share data with others on your network or with people who have user accounts on your computer, you can put the data in the related Public folder. It's often best, for instance, to put all of the music you own in the Public Music folder; you can then access that music from anywhere on your network.

1 Locate the folder that contains the data to move. (It may be on a networked computer.)

2 Select the data. You can hold down the Shift or Ctrl key while selecting to select multiple files or folders.

3 From the Home tab, click Move To, and then Choose Location.

4 Select the folder to move the data to.

5 Click Move.

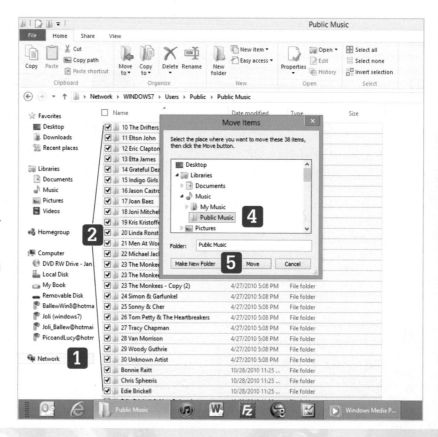

HOT TIP: Often, your new Windows 8 computer will have more hard drive space and a faster processor than any other (older) computer on your network. Thus, it may be best to move data you share to it, such as music, pictures and videos.

SEE ALSO: If you don't want to move data to public folders, you can share your personal folders instead. Refer to Chapter 12 to learn how.

1 Get to know Windows 8

Introduction

Congratulations on the acquisition of Windows 8! Whether you have upgraded your existing system, purchased a new Windows 8 desktop computer or laptop, or purchased the new Microsoft Surface or other compatible tablet, you'll learn how to use it here.

In this chapter, you'll learn how to bypass the Lock screen and log on, how to navigate the Start screen and find apps, and how to access and use 'Charms'. After that you'll learn how to access to the familiar Desktop, Explorer windows, the Taskbar and so on. Before we start though, you need to find out what kind of device you own and learn some of the Windows 8-specific terms you'll see in this book.

Know your device

There are many different types of device that can run Windows 8, including tablets, netbooks, laptops and desktop computers. It's important to know what kind of device you own and what edition of Windows 8 is installed on it, so that you'll know which features of the Windows 8 operating system are available to you.

- Simple tablet – a simple tablet generally runs Windows 8 RT and offers access to the Start screen and the various apps, and you can get more apps from the Store. You can connect to wireless networks, access and play media and games, and use other tablet-specific features.

- Desktop PC or laptop – computers run a full version of Windows 8, and you'll have access to all of the features mentioned for tablets, plus everything you'd expect in a computer, including the ability to add hardware and install software.
- High-end tablet – these tablets run a full version of Windows 8, but you may or may not have access to a physical keyboard, USB ports and other desktop or laptop hardware.

HOT TIP: Some tablets offer only a touch screen and not a physical keyboard. Desktop computers, laptops and high-end tablets may offer keyboard, mouse *and* touch.

Understand new Windows 8 terms

There are a few terms to understand before you jump in to Windows 8. You'll see these terms throughout the book.

1 Lock screen – you must bypass this Lock screen to unlock the computer by inputting your unique password, picture password or PIN.

2 Start screen – the Start screen is what appears after you unlock the computer. It holds tiles that you use to open apps. You saw the Start screen on the previous page.

3 App – a simple program that enables you to do something quickly and easily, like check email, send a message, check the weather or surf the Internet. Apps offer less functionality than their counterparts, the desktop apps, but are easier to use and more streamlined. Here is the Internet Explorer app.

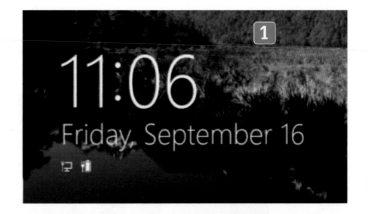

? DID YOU KNOW?

You can right-click an empty area of the Start screen to access all of the available apps. If you use a touch screen, flick upwards from the bottom instead.

4 Desktop apps – these are the traditional programs you may already be familiar with. Desktop apps are fully fledged programs like Paint, Notepad, Windows Media Player, Internet Explorer and similar third-party programs such as Adobe Reader. They open on the Desktop. Here is the Internet Explorer Desktop app.

5 Desktop – the Desktop is the traditional computing environment complete with Taskbar, Desktop background, shortcuts to programs and so on. If you've ever used a computer you've used the Desktop.

? DID YOU KNOW?

Some applications have two versions. As you have seen, there is an Internet Explorer *app* that is available from the Start screen, and an Internet Explorer *Desktop app* available from the Desktop.

🔥 HOT TIP: We believe the majority of Desktop apps are on their way out and that new, more streamlined Start screen-type apps will eventually take their place. Thus, when there are two versions of an app available (such as is the case with Internet Explorer), use the app available from the Start screen.

Understand your account options

When you turned on your Windows 8 device the very first time, you were prompted to create and/or log in with a Microsoft Account. In most instances, this is an email account you already have that ends in live.com or hotmail.com, but it can be something else. If you opted not to do this, then you created a local account. We suggest you use a Microsoft account, as is shown here.

Your account

Joli Ballew
joli_ballew@hotmail.com

Your saved passwords for apps, websites, and networks won't sync until you trust this PC.
Trust this PC

You can switch to a local account, but your settings won't sync between the PCs you use.

Switch to a local account

More account settings online

- Local account – a personal account you use to log on to your Windows 8 computer that is associated only with that computer. Your account settings and preferences can't 'follow' you from one Windows 8 computer to another like a Microsoft account can.

- Microsoft account – a global account you use to log in to your Windows 8 computer. When you use this kind of account, Windows 8 will automatically configure certain apps with personalised information and your preferences and settings will be available no matter what Internet-enabled Windows 8 computer you log on to.

 HOT TIP: It's never too late to switch from a local account to a Microsoft account. See Chapter 3 to learn how.

Log in to Windows 8

The Lock screen appears when you turn on or wake up your Windows 8 computer. You must bypass the Lock screen before you can use your computer.

1 If you have a touch screen, use your finger to swipe upwards from the bottom.

2 If you have a physical keyboard do any of the following:

   a. Swipe upwards with the mouse.

   b. Tap the Space bar.

   c. Click anywhere on the screen.

3 Type your password and tap Enter on the keyboard, or type your password and tap or click the right-facing arrow.

4 The Start screen appears.

? **DID YOU KNOW?**

You can tap or click the icon that looks like an eye that appears in the Password window after you've entered the password to see the actual characters (instead of the dots that appear by default).

▶ **SEE ALSO:** Refer to Chapter 2 to learn how to replace your password with a numeric PIN.

Explore the Start screen

Once you gain access to the Start screen, your computer is ready to use. Note the items available there and understand that your Start screen will look different from ours.

1 Position your mouse at the bottom of the screen; a scroll bar appears to allow access to apps that run off the screen on the right.

2 If you click or tap a tile, the related app opens.

3 To return to the Start screen from any app:

   a. Move the cursor to the bottom left corner of the screen and click the Start screen thumbnail that appears.

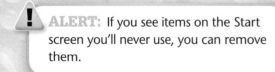

ALERT: If you see items on the Start screen you'll never use, you can remove them.

b. Tap the Windows key on the keyboard.

c. On a touch screen, from the middle of the right side of the screen, flick with your right thumb inwards. Tap the Start 'charm' that appears.

 HOT TIP: To view all of your apps, right-click an empty area of the Start screen and click All Apps. On a touch screen, flick up from the bottom.

 ALERT: If you have a tablet that does not have a physical keyboard, you'll have to rely on 'touch' to navigate the device. We'll offer tips and techniques for doing so throughout this book.

Access charms

Charms enable you to configure settings, share information, view devices, search for data and, as you know, access the Start screen. You can access the charms in many ways.

- Using touch, place your thumb in the middle of the right side of the screen and flick left (inwards).
- On a keyboard, use the key combination Windows key + C.
- On the screen, move the cursor to the bottom right corner, and when the transparent charms appear, move the cursor upwards.

Explore charms

There are five charms. What you see when you click each one may differ depending on what you're doing when you click it. For instance, if you click the Share charm while on the Start screen, you'll be notified there's nothing available to share there. If you click the Share charm while in Maps, you can share the location or directions you've looked up with others via email or other options.

1 Search – to open the Search window where you can type what you're looking for. Note the categories: Apps, Settings, Files.

2 Share – to share something with others, such as a map to a location.

3 Start – to access the Start screen.

4 Devices – to access devices that can be used with the open app, window or program.

5 Settings – to access settings available with the open screen, app, program and so on. You'll use this charm to join networks, change the volume, shut down the computer and more.

HOT TIP: From the Settings charm, click or tap Change PC settings to access the PC Settings screen. You can make changes to your computer there including creating a PIN, changing the Lock screen picture, adding users and so on.

Access the traditional Desktop

The Start screen offers a Desktop tile. This is the tile you use to access the familiar, traditional, computing environment you're used to (if you've used a computer before, that is).

1. Use any method to access the Start screen if you aren't already on it. (You can tap the Windows key on a keyboard.)

2. From the Start screen, click or tap Desktop.

3. Note the Desktop features:
   a. the Recycle Bin
   b. the Taskbar
   c. the Internet Explorer icon
   d. the File Explorer icon
   e. the Notification area

? DID YOU KNOW?

Note the keyboard icon on the Taskbar. You can tap or click this icon to bring up the keyboard when you need it. (If you don't see it, right-click the Taskbar, click Toolbars, and click Touch Keyboard.)

! ALERT: The Start button is no longer available on the Taskbar. If you'd like to access something similar to it, press the Windows key + X key combination.

Open File Explorer

File Explorer enables you to navigate the data on your hard drive. You can access your documents, music, pictures, videos and so on from one window. File Explorer also offers a 'ribbon' where you can perform tasks on data you select. For example, if you select a picture, the option to Print is available from the Share tab.

1 Tabs – tap or click to access options related to the tab's title.

2 Tab commands – tap or click the commands as desired. If a command is greyed out, it can't be used.

3 Libraries – tap or click any library title to view the data you've stored there.

4 Favorites – tap or click any item under Favorites to access data in the folder.

5 Search – type keywords in the Search window to locate specific data in a folder.

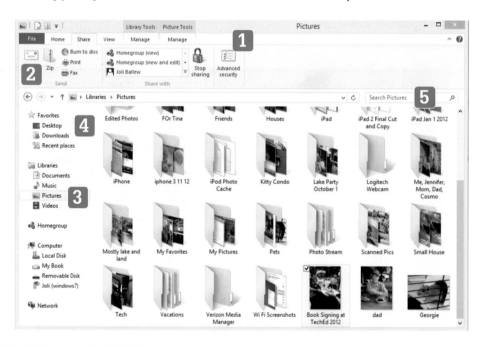

? DID YOU KNOW?
File Explorer used to be called Windows Explorer.

🔥 HOT TIP: When saving data, always save it to a related folder or library. Save pictures in the Pictures library, music in the Music library and so on.

Explore touch techniques

If your tablet does not have a physical keyboard, you'll rely on touch techniques to perform tasks, access data, type and so on. Although you'll learn more techniques as you work through this book, here are the more common ones.

1 Flick up from the bottom to access additional commands and features specific to the open app or window. Here's what you see when you flick upwards in Maps.

2 Flick from the middle of the left side of the screen inwards to move from one open app to another. When you do, one app slides in and the other slides out.

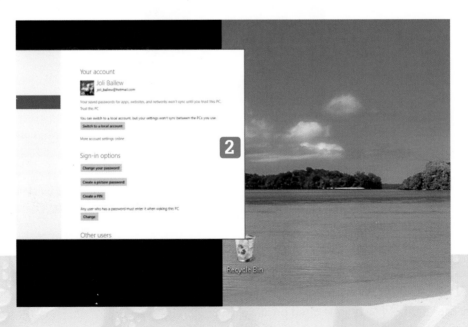

3 Flick from the middle of the right side of the screen inwards to access charms.

4 Tap any item to open it; tap and hold any item to select it; tap, hold and drag downwards a little to perform other tasks (such as to move an item).

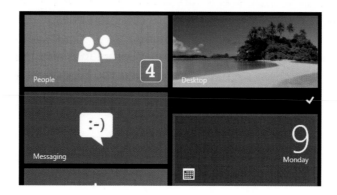

5 Double-tap an item on the Desktop to open it.

6 Tap and hold an icon on the Desktop to access the contextual menu.

? DID YOU KNOW?

The tap-and-hold technique often produces what a traditional right-click does. A double-tap is like a double-click using a mouse. Likewise, tap-hold-and-drag is similar to holding down the mouse button and dragging an item.

Shut down Windows

Your Windows 8 computer will go to sleep after a specific amount of idle time. When this actually happens depends on several factors including what power configuration you've selected and if the tablet or laptop is plugged in or running on batteries. The sleep state is quite efficient and doesn't use much energy, so it's often okay to let the computer go to sleep instead of turning it off each time you have finished using it. However, there will be times when you want to turn off the computer or tablet completely.

1 Access the charms and click or tap Settings.

2 Click or tap Power.

3 Click or tap Shut down.

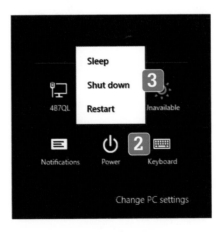

! ALERT: During aircraft takeoffs and landings, you'll be prompted to turn off all devices. You can't just let them go to sleep.

🔥 HOT TIP: If you are relocating a desktop computer, turn it off before you unplug it.

2 Personalise Windows 8

Introduction

Now that you are logged on and have explored the Start screen and Desktop, you can start to personalise your Windows 8 computer. You can create a PIN for logging on, choose a new picture for the Lock screen, create shortcuts on the Desktop, explore and configure the Taskbar, and personalise the tiles that appear on the Start screen. This is an excellent way to make sure your computer suits your exact needs, and an even better way to learn about some of the more common configuration screens.

As you work through the exercises here you'll also learn how to perform specific tasks using a number of methods; this alone is vital knowledge and well worth the time it takes to work through this chapter! Beyond that, while personalising your device you'll also learn many of the mouse, keyboard and touch techniques you'll have to become familiar with to use your computer or tablet effectively. This is a brilliant place to start!

Create a PIN

When you log in you have to type a password. This can become tiring after a while, especially if you don't have a physical keyboard. Even if you do have a keyboard, typing a password still takes time. You can change your log-in requirements so that you need only enter a numeric personal identification number (PIN) instead.

1 On the Start screen, type PIN. (If you don't have access to a physical keyboard, from the Settings charm, tap Keyboard.)

2 On the right side of the screen, click Settings.

3 Click Create a PIN or change PIN.

ALERT: Because we believe most of our readers will have a physical mouse (or the equivalent hardware on a laptop), we'll use the word *click* when we want you to click something with it. If you don't have a physical mouse, you'll need to tap the item instead. (Likewise, a double-click with a mouse is the same as a double-tap with your finger.)

4. Type your current password, click OK, and then enter the desired PIN and confirm.

5. Click Finish.

Create a PIN

A PIN is a quick, convenient way to sign in to this PC by using a 4-digit code.

Enter PIN   ••••

4

Confirm PIN   ••••|

5 Finish   Cancel

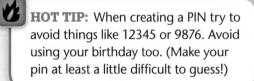

HOT TIP: When creating a PIN try to avoid things like 12345 or 9876. Avoid using your birthday too. (Make your pin at least a little difficult to guess!)

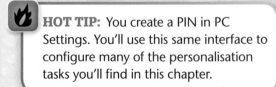

HOT TIP: You create a PIN in PC Settings. You'll use this same interface to configure many of the personalisation tasks you'll find in this chapter.

Change the picture on the Lock screen

You can change the picture that appears on the Lock screen from the same PC Settings interface you used when you created a PIN. As you'll learn here, there is more than one way to open the PC Settings window.

1 At the Start screen, click your user name in the top right corner.

2 Click Change account picture. (This is simply another way to open the PC Settings interface.)

3 In the left pane, click Personalize.

4 In the right pane, click Lock screen.

5 Click one of the images provided or click Browse to locate a picture you'd like to use.

? DID YOU KNOW?

PC Settings isn't technically an app, and it's not a window either. Most people refer to the group of PC Settings commands as an 'interface' or a 'hub'.

? DID YOU KNOW?

You can type just about anything at the Start screen and find what you're looking for under one of the categories shown under the Search window.

Choose Lock screen apps

You may have noticed after using your Windows 8 computer for a while that a few app icons appear on the Lock screen (and they sometimes have numbers with them). By default these include Messaging, Mail and Calendar. Numbers appear when new information is available, such as new email or a new message. You can add more icons if desired and remove the ones you don't want.

1 From the PC Settings interface, click Personalize.

2 In the right pane, click Lock screen.

3 Scroll down to the Lock screen apps section and click a + sign.

4 Choose an app to add.

5 To remove an app icon from the Lock screen, click the app icon and then click Don't show quick status here.

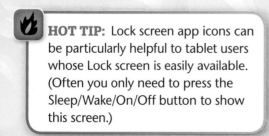

HOT TIP: So far you've explored the Personalize and Users categories in the left pane of the PC Settings interface. Note how many other categories are available (including Notifications, General, Devices and so on).

HOT TIP: Lock screen app icons can be particularly helpful to tablet users whose Lock screen is easily available. (Often you only need to press the Sleep/Wake/On/Off button to show this screen.)

Personalise the Start screen background

When you set up your Windows 8 computer, you were able to choose the colour of the Start screen's background. You can change it again from the PC Settings interface. You'll learn to do that here while you also learn a new way to open the PC Settings hub.

1 Bring up the charms and click Settings. (You can use the keyboard shortcut Windows key + C, flick in from the right side of the screen using your thumb, or position the cursor in the bottom right corner of the screen.)

2 Click Change PC settings.

3 In the left pane click Personalize; in the right pane click Start screen. The right pane is shown here.

4 Move the slider to the desired colour and click your favoured design.

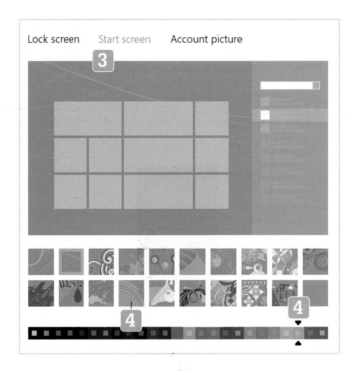

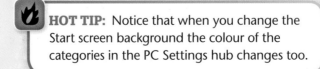

? DID YOU KNOW?

If you use a Microsoft account to log in to your Windows 8 computer, and if you make changes to how your computer looks as outlined in this chapter, then when you log on to any other Windows 8 computer or tablet with that same Microsoft account, those changes will be applied there too.

🔥 HOT TIP: Notice that when you change the Start screen background the colour of the categories in the PC Settings hub changes too.

Reposition apps on the Start screen

As you use your computer, you'll quickly learn which apps you use the most and which you use the least. You may want to move the apps you use regularly to the left side of the Start screen and the apps you use less frequently to the right.

1 If you use a mouse:

   a. Left-click the app to move and hold down the left mouse button.

   b. Drag the app to its new location.

   c. Drop it there.

2 If you use your finger on a touch screen:

   a. Tap and hold the app tile.

   b. Drag it to its new location.

   c. Drop it there.

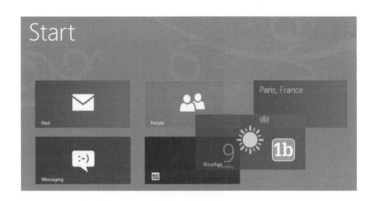

? DID YOU KNOW?

If a number appears on a tile on the Start screen, it means that there is new information there or that the app needs your attention. For instance, a number on the Store icon means an update is available for an app you own.

! ALERT: It may take some practice to learn how to reposition an app's tile with your finger. Sometimes it helps to tap, hold and drag *downwards* first (all in a fairly quick and fluid motion), and then drag the tile to the desired location *after* it's been moved down from its current position.

Make app tiles larger or smaller

Some tiles are small and square, and others are larger and rectangular. Currently you can make any rectangular tile smaller (and then larger again). You cannot resize tiles that are natively square.

1 At the Start screen, right-click the Desktop tile. Note a tick mark appears by it.

2 Click Smaller.

3 Repeat and click Larger.

! ALERT: If you select multiple tiles, the option to make the tiles larger or smaller disappears. In this case, click Clear selection and start again.

HOT TIP: If you're using a touch screen, to select a tile and enable the tick mark (and to show the options at the bottom of the screen to make the tile larger or smaller), tap, hold and drag downwards. A tick mark will appear when you've done this correctly (and it may take some practice).

Turn live tiles off or on

Live tiles flip every second or two to show ever-changing information as it relates to the app. For example, the Photos tile will flip through pictures you've stored on your hard drive or on connected social networks, and the Sports tile will show the latest sports headlines obtained from the Internet. If you spend a lot of time at the Start screen, all of this flipping can become distracting. Alternatively, you may want to enable Live tiles for apps you use often, like Calendar, so you can keep up with your latest appointments without having to open the app itself.

1 At the Start screen, right-click the Photos tile. Note a tick mark appears by it. (On a touch screen, tap, hold and drag downwards.)

2 Note the option to turn the live tile off (shown here), or to turn it on (not shown).

3 Click the desired choice, and then repeat with other tiles as desired.

🔥 HOT TIP: Not all tiles are live.

🔥 HOT TIP: If you select a tile and then change your mind, just right-click it or drag it downwards according to your system to deselect it.

❓ DID YOU KNOW?
If you want to remove a tile from the Start screen but you don't want to uninstall it from your computer, click Unpin from Start. You can always add it back later.

Add a tile to the Start screen

There are more windows, apps, programs and applications available than those that appear on the Start screen by default. There's the Calculator for instance, and Windows Media Player, Control Panel, Windows Explorer and Notepad, to name a few. You can add any item to the Start screen to have easier access to it.

1 Right-click an empty area of the Start screen. On a touch screen, flick upwards from the bottom of the screen.

2 Click All apps.

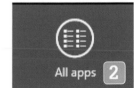

3 Right-click (or tap, hold and drag downwards) an item you'd like to add. We suggest File Explorer, but you may want to add Calculator, Help and Support, or WordPad.

4 From the bar that appears at the bottom of the page (not shown) click Pin to Start.

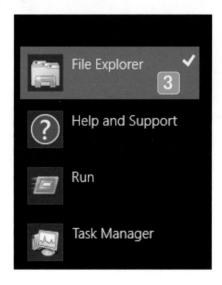

5 Return to the Start screen and locate the new tile. It will be placed on the far right.

DID YOU KNOW?
You can open an app from the All Apps screen by clicking it once.

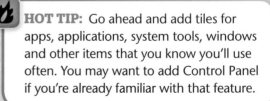
HOT TIP: Go ahead and add tiles for apps, applications, system tools, windows and other items that you know you'll use often. You may want to add Control Panel if you're already familiar with that feature.

Remove a tile from the Start screen

You remove an unwanted tile from the Start screen by selecting it and then choosing Unpin from Start. If you like, you can select multiple tiles to remove.

1 Right-click or tap, hold and drag downwards on any tile you'd like to remove.

2 Repeat as desired to select additional tiles.

3 Click or tap Unpin from Start.

HOT TIP: After you've removed unwanted tiles, reposition what's left by dragging the remaining tiles to the desired positions.

? DID YOU KNOW?
When you remove a tile from the Start screen you don't uninstall it. You can always access it (and even add it back) from the All Apps screen.

Personalise the Desktop

If you've been reading in sequence, you know that the Start screen is the starting point for Windows 8, and that you click or tap tiles on that screen to open apps and programs to perform tasks. You know that the Desktop is a tile available on the Start screen, and that selecting this tile will open the computing environment you're probably already familiar with (the Desktop). Once you're at the Desktop, you can personalise it to suit your specific needs and preferences.

1 From the Start screen, click or tap Desktop.

2 Right-click (or long tap) an empty area of the Desktop and click Personalize.

3 Note the options. You can:

   a. select a new theme
   b. change the Desktop background
   c. configure Sounds
   d. select a screen saver.

4 Make changes as desired.

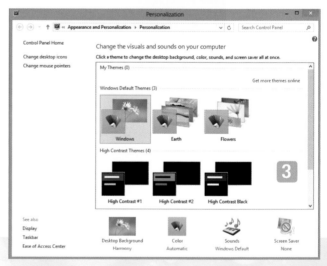

HOT TIP: Try High Contrast Black or High Contrast White if you have a visual impairment.

? DID YOU KNOW?

A screen saver is a moving graphic that appears on your screen when the computer has been idle for a pre-set amount of time. This keeps the monitor healthy by preventing 'burn-in' and enables you to secure the computer with a screen saver and password.

Create a shortcut for a folder or library on the Desktop

If you work at the Desktop regularly you can create shortcuts there for folders and libraries you use often. This makes it easier to open those items when you need them. You can locate these items in File Explorer.

1 From the Start screen, click Desktop.

2 On the Desktop, from the Taskbar, click the folder icon. This opens File Explorer and gives access to your Libraries.

> ▶ **SEE ALSO:** To add shortcuts to programs and Desktop applications, refer to the next section.

3 To add a shortcut to any library or folder:

   a. Right-click the item. (On a touch screen, use a long tap.)

   b. Click Send to.

   c. Click Desktop (create shortcut). Note the option to Pin to Start (that's the Start screen).

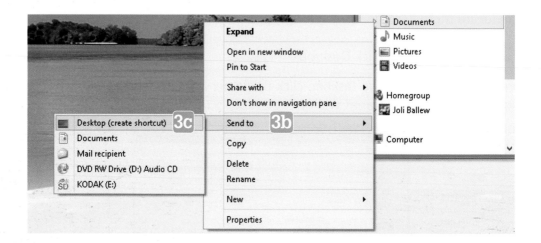

4 Repeat as desired.

WHAT DOES THIS MEAN?

Library: A container that offers access to two or more folders. The Pictures library offers access to both your personal Pictures folder and the Public Pictures folder, for instance. You can create new and manage existing libraries. (See Chapter 11 for more information.)

Create a shortcut for a program, accessory, system tool and more

You have to locate the item you want to add to the Desktop before you can right-click (or long tap) it to access the Send to command. The easiest way to do this is to use the Start screen.

1️⃣ Right-click an empty area of the Start screen and click All apps. (Flick upwards on a touch screen.)

2️⃣ Use the scroll bar to move to the right of the screen and right-click the application, tool, accessory or program to add.

3️⃣ Click Open file location. (If you don't see this, you can't create a shortcut for it.)

4️⃣ Right-click (long tap) the item and click Send to.

5️⃣ Click Desktop (create shortcut).

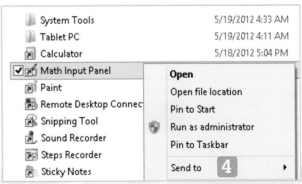

? DID YOU KNOW?

You can't add shortcuts for any of the Start screen apps to the Desktop. You can only add shortcuts for Desktop apps, Windows Accessories, Windows System tools and similar items.

🔥 HOT TIP: You don't always have to add a shortcut on the Desktop. You can pin the item to the Desktop's Taskbar instead. You may see this option along with the Send to command in a contextual menu, or you may not. It depends on what you're trying to add.

Add an item to the Taskbar

If you'd rather not clutter up your Desktop with shortcuts, you can opt to add icons for items to the Taskbar. This is called 'pinning' an item. You already know you can choose Pin to Start to add tiles to the Start screen. Another option is Pin to taskbar.

1 From the Start screen (or the All apps screen) right-click an item you'd like to add to the Taskbar.

2 Click Pin to taskbar. If you don't see this option, it can't be pinned.

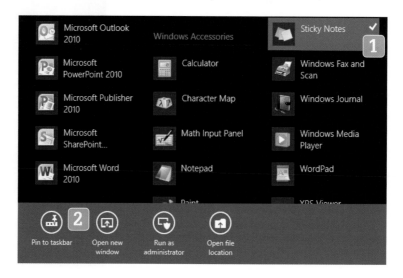

3 Repeat as desired, and then note the new items that are pinned.

HOT TIP: As you get to know Windows 8 and learn which Desktop apps you use most, pin them to the Taskbar. You may want to pin Windows Media Player, Sticky Notes, Help and Support and others.

HOT TIP: Once an item is pinned to the Taskbar, you only have to click or tap it once to open it.

Configure Taskbar properties

You can configure the Taskbar so that it's locked in place and can't be dragged elsewhere, you can auto-hide the Taskbar when you aren't using it, and more.

1 Right-click an empty area of the Taskbar and click Properties.

2 Make changes as desired and click OK.

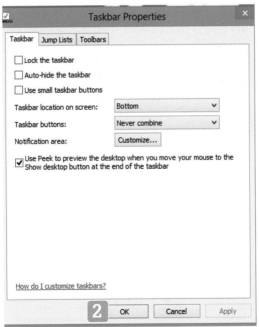

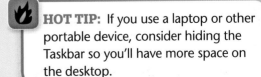

? DID YOU KNOW?
You can drag an unlocked Taskbar to the top, left or right side of the screen.

🔥 HOT TIP: If you use a laptop or other portable device, consider hiding the Taskbar so you'll have more space on the desktop.

Choose which Desktop icons appear

By default, the Recycle Bin is the only icon on the Desktop. You can add icons for commonly used items from the Personalization options in the Control Panel.

1 Right-click an empty area of the Desktop and click Personalize.

2 Click Change desktop icons.

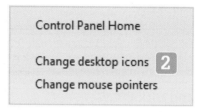

3 Place a tick by the items you'd like to add to the Desktop and click OK.

HOT TIP: Remember, in many cases, a long tap is equivalent to a right-click of a mouse.

HOT TIP: Continue to explore the various personalisation options as time allows. When you're ready, continue to the next chapter.

3 Use the basic apps

Introduction

If you've ever used a high-end smart phone, i-device, android tablet or Windows phone, you've used apps. Apps are programs that enable you to do something quickly and without much effort, such as check the current weather, get directions and read email. Almost all apps use the Internet to obtain their information.

In this chapter you'll learn how to use some of the more basic apps available from the Windows 8 Start screen. You'll learn how to view recent weather updates, for instance, and how to locate something in Maps. If you use a Microsoft account, you'll learn how to access your free, personal SkyDrive space, where you can store files for safe keeping. In later chapters you'll learn how to use most of the other apps not introduced here (such as Mail, Messaging, Music, Photos and Video).

Know why you need a Microsoft account

We've already encouraged you several times to get (or use or configure) a Microsoft account. If you haven't done so because you're still on the fence about it, here is a list of reasons why you should.

- You can use your favourite email address as your Microsoft account.
- You need a Microsoft account to use the Store. This is where you get more apps.

- You can upload, access and share your photos, documents and other files from places like SkyDrive, Facebook or Flickr.

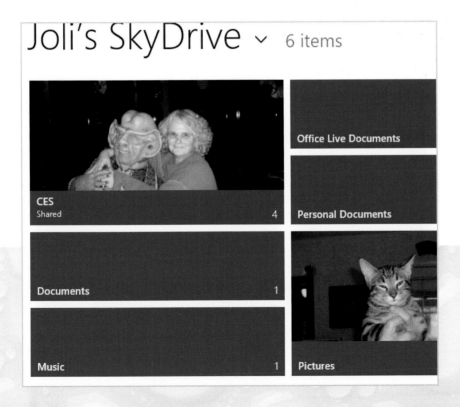

- You can log on to any Internet-connected Windows 8 computer (or tablet) with your Microsoft account. When you do, the personal settings you have already created on another Windows 8 computer are synced to it, including your themes, language preferences, browser favourites, browser history and apps.

- The apps you acquire in the Windows Store can be used on any Windows 8 PC you log in to with your Microsoft account.

 HOT TIP: You can sign up for a free Microsoft account at https://signup.live.com/. Alternatively, you can use your existing email address or obtain a new one as outlined in the next section.

? DID YOU KNOW?
You'll get a free personalised webpage when you sign up for a Microsoft account. There you can access your email, link other accounts, access Messenger and SkyDrive, and personalise the page with content, colours, themes and more.

Switch to a Microsoft account

After you've obtained a Microsoft account, or decided you want to use an existing email account as your Microsoft account, you can switch to it. You need to access PC Settings to get started.

1 Bring up the charms and click Settings.

2 Click Change PC settings.

3 Tap or click Users.

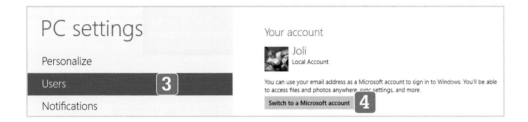

4 Tap or click Switch to a Microsoft account.

5 Enter your existing Microsoft account, one you have recently obtained or your favourite email address. You can also get a new email address from this screen.

6 Complete the process as instructed.

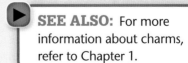 **DID YOU KNOW?**
To access the charms, position your mouse in the bottom right corner of the screen. On a touch screen, swipe in from the middle of the right edge with your thumb or finger.

SEE ALSO: For more information about charms, refer to Chapter 1.

View your local weather

You can easily view your local weather forecast from the Weather app. It's located on the Home screen.

1 From the Start screen, click the Weather tile.

2 Click Allow to let the app learn your location.

3 Note the information offered, and use the scroll bar to view more.

4 To configure additional locations, right-click and click Places. Click the + sign to get started.

Search for a location with Maps

You can use the Maps app to locate a place or get directions from one place to another. By default, Maps will use your current location as the starting point, provided you allow it to access your position when prompted.

1 From the Start screen, click Maps.

2 Right-click or swipe upwards from the bottom to access the available Maps charms.

Show traffic   Map style   My location   Directions

3 Explore the following: **3**

   a. Show traffic – to view the current flow of traffic as green, yellow or red. Green means traffic is moving; red means it's extremely slow.

   b. Map style – to switch from the default Road view to Aerial view.

   c. My location – to have Maps place a diamond on the map to indicate where you are.

   d. Directions – to get directions from one place to another.

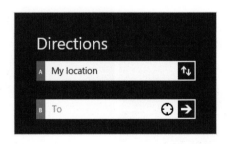

ALERT: You will not be able to view traffic conditions if the traffic where you are is not monitored.

HOT TIP: Click My location, and then click Map style, Aerial view. Zoom in to view a picture of your home, business or location as it appears from the sky!

Read Travel articles

The Travel app is one of the easiest to use, and is packed with information about places you may want to visit or read about. One of the most outstanding features is the ability to explore cities in 360-degree views.

1 From the Start screen, click Travel.

2 Use the scroll bar on the screen or on your mouse to move through the information.

3 Click any item to view it; click the resulting 'back' button to return.

4 Locate the Panoramas section; specifically any item with 360° on it. Click it.

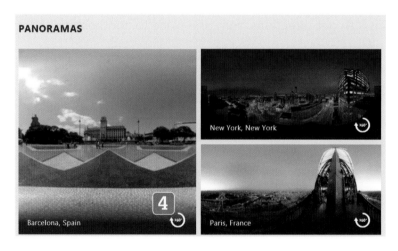

5 Use your finger or mouse to drag on the image to move it around on the screen.

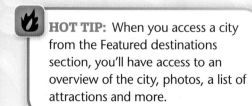

HOT TIP: When you access a city from the Featured destinations section, you'll have access to an overview of the city, photos, a list of attractions and more.

DID YOU KNOW?
While in any app, such as Travel, you can access the previously used app by moving the mouse cursor to the top left corner and clicking. If you use touch only, flick inwards from the left middle edge.

Get the latest sports news and follow a team

Like the Travel app, the Sports app also offers a host of information. There are articles, photos and the ability to add your favourite teams. Once you add those teams you can use the Sports app to follow them easily.

1 From the Start screen, click Sports.

2 Scroll through the available articles, news and photos.

3 On the far right, locate the Favorite Teams section. Click the + sign.

4 Type the team to follow. Repeat as desired. Click Cancel.

5 Note the new entries; you can now click any of these to learn more.

6 Right-click on any Sports app screen to view additional options.

FAVORITE TEAMS

Manchester United
2nd in Premier League
5-2, 15 PTS

Dallas Cowboys
4th in NFC East
2-3,L2

Toronto Maple Leafs
1st in Northeast
0-0

Houston Texans
1st in AFC South
5-1,L1

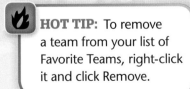

HOT TIP: To remove a team from your list of Favorite Teams, right-click it and click Remove.

DID YOU KNOW?
You can position your mouse in the bottom right corner of the Sports app and click the dash that appears to access a list of available categories (such as Top Story, News, Schedule and Favorite Teams).

View your personal calendar

The Calendar app lets you input calendar data, which is synced with your Microsoft account, which in turn enables you to receive alerts about events from any device that can receive them. You can view the Calendar in many ways.

1 From the Start screen, click Calendar.

2 Right-click with a mouse or flick upwards from the bottom of the screen with your finger to access the Calendar's charms.

3 Explore Day, Week and Month by clicking them each once.

4 Click any day or time slot to create a new appointment.

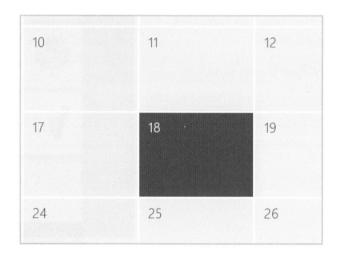

 DID YOU KNOW?
Use a Microsoft account and you can view your calendar from almost anywhere. It's on the web at https://calendar.live.com/.

HOT TIP: The Calendar tile on the Start screen is live. This means that as appointment and event dates get near, the tile will show the information on the Start screen.

Create a new event in Calendar

You can create a new event in Calendar simply by clicking the + sign from the Calendar charms or by clicking once on any date or time. You can add many types of information. To see all of the options, click Show More in the new event window. As the time draws near, the Calendar tile will show the event and details. (Make sure you click the Save icon to save the events you create!)

- What, where and the time the event is to take place.
- What calendar you should use if you have several.
- If the event recurs or not.
- A description.
- A list of people to invite.
- Your availability status.
- A reminder.

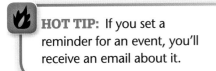

HOT TIP: If you set a reminder for an event, you'll receive an email about it.

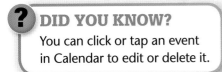

DID YOU KNOW?
You can click or tap an event in Calendar to edit or delete it.

Explore your SkyDrive space

When you set up a Microsoft account you are given some free space on Microsoft's Internet servers to store some of your files, pictures and other data. That space is called SkyDrive. There is a SkyDrive app on the Start screen.

1 From the Start screen, click SkyDrive.

2 Note the categories. You may see Documents, Music, Pictures and others.

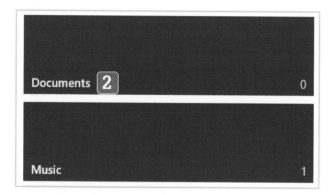

3 Click any category to see what's inside. If subfolders exist, explore those too.

WHAT DOES THIS MEAN?

SkyDrive: This term means that you have access to a *drive* (like a hard drive) in the *sky* (which is actually the Internet). Because the Internet is often represented in technical documentation as a cloud, the word sky fits the context.

? DID YOU KNOW?

You can access data you've saved to SkyDrive from any Internet-enabled computer. It does not have to be a Windows 8 computer.

? DID YOU KNOW?

A number on any category title tells you how many items are in the folder.

Upload a file to SkyDrive

As with other apps, the SkyDrive app offers charms. You access the charms using a right-click or by flicking upwards with your finger. One of the options there is Upload. You use this command to add files to SkyDrive from your computer.

1 Navigate to the folder in SkyDrive you'd like to add files to.

2 Access the charms, and then click Upload.

3 Browse to the files to add and click them. (You can hold down the Ctrl key to select multiple files.)

4 Click Add to SkyDrive.

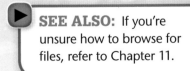

SEE ALSO: If you're unsure how to browse for files, refer to Chapter 11.

DID YOU KNOW?

One of the charms available in SkyDrive is New Folder. Create new folders to organise the data you keep there.

Obtain a new app from the Store

You can get additional apps from the Store, available from the Start screen. You'll need a Microsoft account to use the Store, even though many apps are free.

1 From the Start screen, click Store.

2 Scroll, browse, navigate and explore the items in the Store using techniques you've already learned in this chapter, such as scrolling and clicking.

3 Locate an item to install and click it.

4 Read the information on the app's Details page and, if desired, click Install.

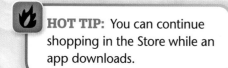
HOT TIP: You can continue shopping in the Store while an app downloads.

ALERT: Many apps are free, but many you'll have to pay for. If prompted to pay for an app, read the instructions for doing so, and set up the required payment account.

Open and use a new app

Once a new app is installed, you can find it on the Start screen. It will be on the far right side, although you can move it somewhere else if you want to.

1 From the Start screen, locate the new app.

2 Click or tap the app tile to open it.

3 Read any directions, input required information and so on, and then use the app as directed. Here, you are instructed to slice a piece of fruit to get started.

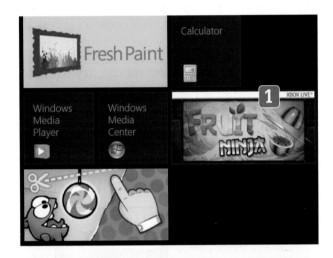

 HOT TIP: You can unpin an app from the Start screen if you don't want it there, but if you know you won't use the app opt to uninstall it instead. Right-click the app tile on the Start screen to access both of these options.

ALERT: Some apps offer in-app purchases. This means you can pay for more 'bombs', 'lives' and various additional features. But be careful: this can get expensive!

? DID YOU KNOW?
When you leave an app to do something else, the app stops where it is; it 'pauses'. It does not continue to use system resources, and generally you don't have to 'start over' when you come back to the app, for instance when playing a game.

Move among open apps

So far you've learned several ways to move among apps, including using a flicking motion inwards from the left side of a touch screen to access the previously used app. You also know you can tap the Windows key or move the cursor to the bottom left corner of the screen and click once to access the Start menu, and thus the available list of apps. There are other ways to explore.

If you have a keyboard and mouse, try these techniques while on any screen or in any app:

1 Hold down the Windows key and press the Tab key to show thumbnails of each open app. Press Tab repeatedly until you get to the app you want to use, then let go of both. Here the Desktop is open, and Calendar is selected as the desired app on the left.

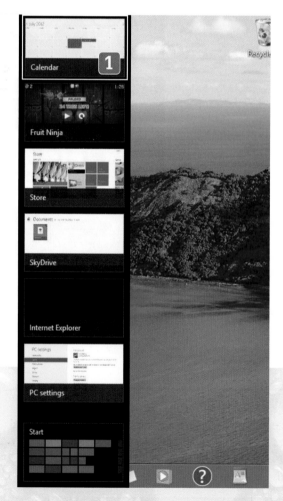

2 Hold down the Alt key and press the Tab key to show a row of open apps. Press Tab repeatedly until you get to the app you want to use, then let go. Here SkyDrive is open and selected. You'll have to press Tab to move to another app.

3 Position your mouse in the top left corner of the screen to view and click the last used app. Drag the mouse downwards slowly to view the other available apps.

HOT TIP: The left to right flicking motion from the left edge of a touch screen is the best option for moving among open apps on a tablet.

? DID YOU KNOW?

Some tablets offer USB ports. You may be able to connect a USB mouse. Likewise, if Bluetooth is an option, you may be able to connect a Bluetooth keyboard.

4 Use Internet Explorer

Introduction

You use Internet Explorer to access the Internet and browse websites. This is why it's called a *web browser*. You'll learn how to use Internet Explorer in this chapter.

Before we start though, it's important to understand that there are two versions of Internet Explorer (IE) available in Windows 8. The IE *app* is available from the Start screen. It offers limited functionality, but is streamlined to offer a clean and efficient web browsing experience. You should use this version when you want to visit your favourite websites and do some basic web surfing. The *IE Desktop app* is the fully functional version of IE that you may already be familiar with. It offers what the IE app offers and much, much more, including the ability to save a list of Favorites, use the familiar tabbed browsing features and print a webpage, among other things.

So, let's start with the IE app you'll find on the Start screen, get to know that version, and then move on to the IE Desktop app. You can decide which you'd prefer to use after exploring both.

Understand the versions of IE

You learned in the introduction that there are two versions of IE. One is an app on the Start screen, and one is a Desktop app. Here are some of the major differences between them.

- Any time you click a link in an email, message, document and so on, the IE app will open. It is the default app.

- The IE app is available from the Start screen but the Desktop version is not (although you can add it there).

- The IE app is a better option on tablets and computers with small screens than its full-version counterpart, because the IE app was built to offer a full-screen browsing experience in a limited space.

Internet Explorer

- The IE Desktop app is a traditional application that looks and acts much like its predecessor. It is fully extensible with third-party add-ons.

- You will have to switch from the IE app to the Desktop version whenever a webpage won't function properly, such as when an add-on, Java, Flash or other technologies are required.

 HOT TIP: You can quickly pin any website to the Start screen from inside the IE app.

 DID YOU KNOW?
View on the Desktop is an option in the IE app. This means you can use the app until you need the other version, and then switch to it easily.

Explore the IE app

You open the IE app by clicking or tapping its tile on the Start screen. When the app opens, look for the features listed here. You must right-click or flick upwards from the bottom of a touch screen to access these features. By default, nothing shows on the screen but the website itself.

a. Address bar – here we've navigated to https://twitter.com.

b. Back – use this to return to the previously visited webpage.

c. Refresh – use to reload the webpage.

d. Pin to Start – click to create a tile for the webpage on the Start screen.

e. Page Tools – Click to find something on a page, view the website in the Desktop app and more.

f. Forward – click to move to a previously visited page. This is available only after clicking the Back button.

g. Tabs – click any thumbnail to return to a previously tabbed website. Note the option to remove the thumbnail (X), and the options to open and close tabs (+ and ...).

h. Content – this is the webpage content.

HOT TIP: Click anywhere on the webpage to hide the features shown.

? DID YOU KNOW?

If you position your cursor in the middle of the left or right side of the page, transparent Back and Forward arrows appear.

Visit a website

There are several ways to visit a website, including clicking links on other webpages, in emails and in messages. You can also navigate to a website by typing its name in the Address bar.

1 From the Start screen, click the Internet Explorer tile.

2 Click once in the Address bar. (Right-click if it's not visible.)

3 Type the desired web address.

4 If you've visited the page before, it will appear above the Address bar and you can click it.

5 If not, simply press Enter on the keyboard or click the right-facing arrow.

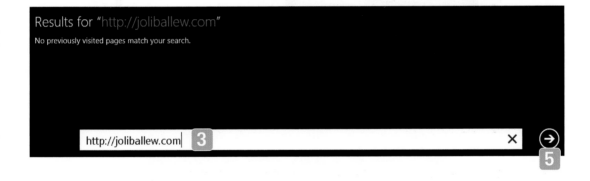

Results for "http://joliballew.com"

No previously visited pages match your search.

http://joliballew.com ✕ →

HOT TIP: Navigate to a second and third website using the Address bar, and then practise using the Back and Forward buttons and arrows.

? DID YOU KNOW?

After you've used the IE app for a while, the app will determine which websites you visit most. Then, when you click inside the Address bar, thumbnails will be available to quickly access those sites.

Manage tabs with the hidden toolbar

You saw the tabs on the hidden toolbar in the previous section. You use these features to manage open websites and to open and close tabs. Before you work through this page, navigate to several websites from the Address bar or using any other method.

1 Right-click the screen.

2 Click the X by any tab to close it.

3 Click the + sign to open a new, blank page, and type the desired address or choose from the thumbnails that appear.

4 Click the three dots (...). Note the options and explore as desired.

? DID YOU KNOW?

If you opt to open a new tab using the InPrivate option (available from the Tab tools), IE won't remember the website in its History list, and won't save anything else related to your visit either.

🔥 HOT TIP: To close all of your open tabs quickly, right-click, click the Tab tools icon (...), and click Close Tabs.

Pin a website to the Start screen

If there's a website you visit often you can pin it to the Start screen. Then you can simply click the tile to open the IE app and go directly to it.

1 Use the IE app to navigate to a website.

2 Right-click if applicable to show the toolbars.

3 Click Pin to Start.

4 If desired, type a new name for the website.

5 Click Pin to Start.

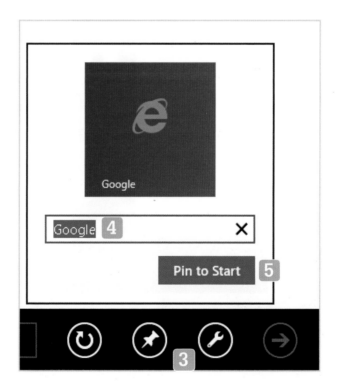

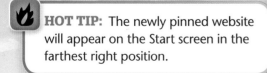

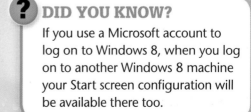

HOT TIP: The newly pinned website will appear on the Start screen in the farthest right position.

? DID YOU KNOW?
If you use a Microsoft account to log on to Windows 8, when you log on to another Windows 8 machine your Start screen configuration will be available there too.

Explore Settings

You can configure settings for IE from the Settings charm. These include the ability to delete your browsing history, enable or disable a website from requesting permission to ask for your physical location and more.

 Open the IE app, and using any method, bring up the charms.

2 Click Settings.

3 Click Internet Options.

4 Explore the options.

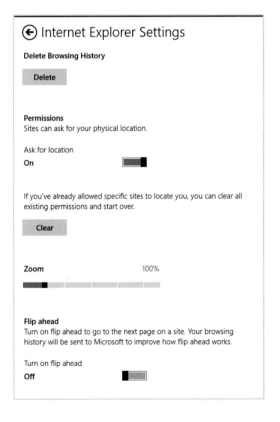

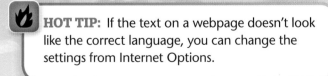

HOT TIP: If the text on a webpage doesn't look like the correct language, you can change the settings from Internet Options.

Explore the IE Desktop app

As you know, Windows 8 comes with another version of IE, the Desktop version. One way to access this version is to first access the Desktop from the Start screen, and once the Desktop opens click the big blue E on the Taskbar, which represents Internet Explorer.

1 To go to a website you want to visit, type the name of the website in the window at the top of the page. This is called the Address bar.

2 Press Enter on the keyboard.

3 Explore these features:

a. Tabs – click any tab to access the related webpage.

b. Home – click to access your configured Home page(s).

c. View Favorites, feeds and history – click to view favourites or to add a webpage as a favourite and more.

d. Tools – click to access all of the available settings.

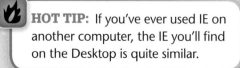

HOT TIP: If you've ever used IE on another computer, the IE you'll find on the Desktop is quite similar.

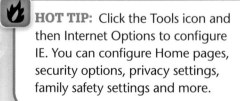

HOT TIP: Click the Tools icon and then Internet Options to configure IE. You can configure Home pages, security options, privacy settings, family safety settings and more.

Use tabs

You can open more than one website at a time in IE. To do this, click the tab that appears to the right of the open webpage. Then type the name of the website you'd like to visit.

1 Open Internet Explorer.

2 Click an empty tab.

3 Type the name of the website you'd like to visit in the Address bar.

4 Press Enter on the keyboard.

? DID YOU KNOW?

When a website name starts with https://, it means it's secure. When purchasing items online, make sure the payment pages have this prefix.

! ALERT: Websites almost always start with http://www.

Set a home page

You can select a single webpage or multiple webpages to be displayed each time you open IE. In fact, there are three options for configuring home pages:

- Use this webpage as your only home page – select this option if you want only one page to serve as your home page.
- Add this webpage to your home page tabs – select this option if you want this page to be one of several home pages.
- Use the current tab set as your home page – select this option if you've opened multiple tabs and you want all of them to be home pages.

1 Use the address bar to locate a webpage (and use the empty tab button to open additional webpages).

2 Right-click the Home icon and click Add or change home page. (Note you have additional choices, including showing various toolbars.)

3 Make a selection using the information provided regarding each option.

4 Click Yes.

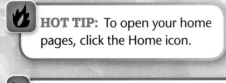 **HOT TIP:** To open your home pages, click the Home icon.

ALERT: You have to locate the webpage before you can assign it as a home page.

▶ **SEE ALSO:** 'Visit a website' earlier in this chapter.

Mark a favourite

Favourites are websites you save links to for accessing more easily at a later time. They differ from home pages because by default they do not open when you start IE. The favourites you save appear in the Favorites Center. You can also save favourites to the Favorites bar, an optional toolbar you can enable in IE.

1 Go to the webpage you want to configure as a favourite.

2 Click the Add to favorites icon. (It's the star.)

3 Click Add to favorites. (To add the website to the Favorites bar, click the arrow beside the Add to favorites option.)

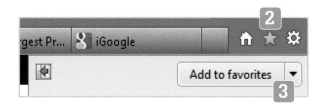
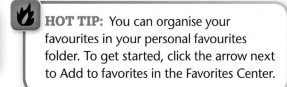
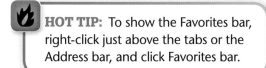

HOT TIP: To show the Favorites bar, right-click just above the tabs or the Address bar, and click Favorites bar.

HOT TIP: You can organise your favourites in your personal favourites folder. To get started, click the arrow next to Add to favorites in the Favorites Center.

Zoom in or out

If you have trouble reading what's on a webpage because the text is too small, use the Page Zoom feature. Page Zoom preserves the fundamental design of the webpage you're viewing. This means that Page Zoom intelligently zooms in on the entire page, which maintains the page's integrity, layout and look.

1 Open Internet Explorer and browse to a webpage.

2 If you have a physical keyboard, use the Ctrl + = and the Ctrl + − combinations to zoom in and out.

3 If you have a touch screen, pinch in and out with two or more fingers.

4 Alternatively you can:

    a. Right-click the area above the tabs and Address bar and place a tick by the Status bar.

    b. Then click the arrow at the right end of the Status bar to zoom to a specific amount.

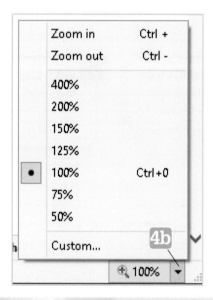

Print a webpage

You can print a webpage in several ways. When you do though, remember that the pictures and ads will be printed too, so you may want to copy the text and paste it into a Word document first.

- The Print icon is available from the Command bar. To show the Command bar right-click just above the tabs and Address bar and place a tick by it. The Command bar and the Print option is shown here.

- The key combination Ctrl + P will bring up the Print dialogue box.

- You can right-click on an empty area of the webpage and click Print from the resulting contextual menu. A long tap on a touch screen works too.

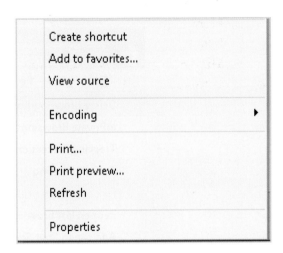

DID YOU KNOW?

You can search from the Address bar. Simply type your keywords there and press Enter on the keyboard.

WHAT DOES THIS MEAN?

There are three menu options under the Print icon:

Print: Clicking Print opens the Print dialogue box where you can configure the page range, select a printer, change page orientation, change print order and choose a paper type. Additional options include print quality, output bins and more. Of course, the choices depend on what your printer offers. If your printer can print only at 300×300 dots per inch, you can't configure it to print at a higher quality.

Print preview: Clicking Print preview opens a window where you can see before you print what the printout will actually look like. You can switch between portrait and landscape views, access the Page Setup dialogue box and more.

Page Setup: Clicking Page Setup opens the Page Setup dialogue box. Here you can select a paper size, source, and create headers and footers. You can also change orientation and margins, all of which is dependent on what features your printer supports.

Clear your browsing history

If you don't want people to be able to snoop around on your computer and find out which sites you've been visiting you'll need to delete your 'browsing history'. Deleting your browsing history lets you remove the information stored on your computer related to your Internet activities.

1 Open Internet Explorer on the Desktop.

2 Click the Alt key on the keyboard if you do not see the menu shown here.

3 Click Tools.

4 Click Delete browsing history.

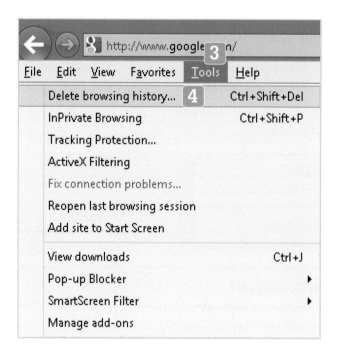

? DID YOU KNOW?

You can also click the Tools icon, Internet Options and, from the General tab, opt to delete your browsing history.

5 Select what to delete, and click Delete. (You may want to keep Preserve Favorites website data that is shown here as selected.)

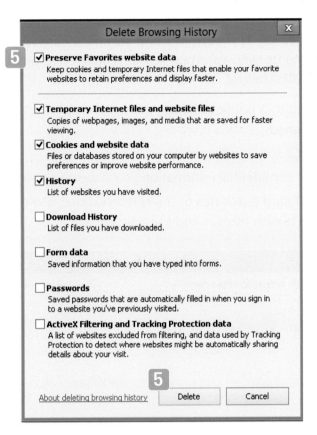

Delete Browsing History

5 ☑ **Preserve Favorites website data**
Keep cookies and temporary Internet files that enable your favorite websites to retain preferences and display faster.

☑ **Temporary Internet files and website files**
Copies of webpages, images, and media that are saved for faster viewing.

☑ **Cookies and website data**
Files or databases stored on your computer by websites to save preferences or improve website performance.

☑ **History**
List of websites you have visited.

☐ **Download History**
List of files you have downloaded.

☐ **Form data**
Saved information that you have typed into forms.

☐ **Passwords**
Saved passwords that are automatically filled in when you sign in to a website you've previously visited.

☐ **ActiveX Filtering and Tracking Protection data**
A list of websites excluded from filtering, and data used by Tracking Protection to detect where websites might be automatically sharing details about your visit.

5

About deleting browsing history | Delete | Cancel

WHAT DOES THIS MEAN?

Temporary Internet Files: Files that have been downloaded and saved in your Temporary Internet Files folder. A snooper could go through these files to see what you've been doing online.

Cookies: Small text files that include data that identifies your preferences when you visit particular websites. Cookies are what allow you to visit, say, www.amazon.com and be greeted with 'Hello <your name>, We have recommendations for you!' Cookies help a site offer you a personalised web experience.

History: The list of websites you've visited and any web addresses you've typed. Anyone can look at your History list to see where you've been.

Form data: Information that's been saved using IE's autocomplete form data functionality. If you don't want forms to be filled out automatically by you or someone else who has access to your PC and user account, delete this.

Passwords: Passwords that were saved using IE autocomplete password prompts.

InPrivate Blocking data: Data that was saved by InPrivate Blocking to detect where websites may be automatically sharing details about your visit.

Stay safe on the Internet

You'll learn how to use Windows Firewall, Windows Defender and other security features later (in Chapter 13). However, much of staying secure when online and surfing the Internet has more to do with common sense. When you're online, make sure you follow the guidelines listed below.

- If you are connecting to a public network, make sure you select Public when prompted by Windows 8.
- Always keep your PCs secure with anti-virus software.
- Limit the amount of confidential information you store on the Internet.
- When making credit card purchases or travel reservations, always make sure the website address starts with https:// and use a secure site.

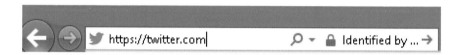

- Always sign out of any secure website you enter.

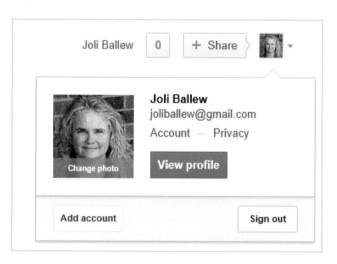

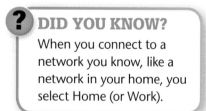

? DID YOU KNOW?

When you connect to a network you know, like a network in your home, you select Home (or Work).

! ALERT: You have to purchase and install your own anti-virus software; it does not come with Windows 8. However, Microsoft Security Essentials is free, and provides anti-virus and anti-malware protection.

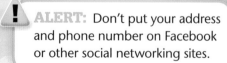

! ALERT: Don't put your address and phone number on Facebook or other social networking sites.

Configure the IE Desktop app as the default

If you'd prefer that the IE Desktop app opens when you click a link in an email, message, document and so on, instead of the simpler IE app, you can configure it in Internet Explorer's settings. Doing so will make the Desktop app the default.

1. Open Internet Explorer on the Desktop.

2. Click the Tools icon, then Internet Options.

3. Click the Programs tab.

4. Click the arrow beside Let Internet Explorer decide.

5. Click Always in Internet Explorer on the desktop.

6. Click OK.

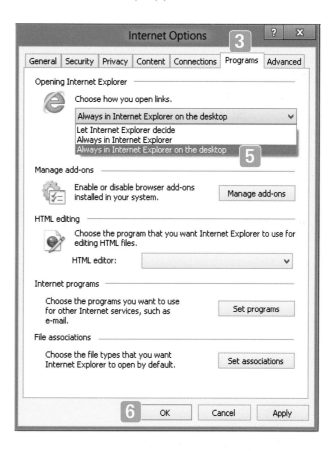

 HOT TIP: While you have the Internet Options dialogue box open, explore the other options available. From the General tab, for instance, you can configure IE to start each time with tabs from the last session (instead of your configured home page(s).)

 DID YOU KNOW?

You can still use the IE app on the Start screen even if you change the defaults as outlined here.

5 Set up and use Mail

Introduction

Mail is an app available from the Start screen that enables you to view, send and receive email, and manage sent, saved and incoming mail using various techniques. It's an app, so it offers minimal features compared with other, full applications such as Windows Live Mail, Microsoft Office Outlook and Mozilla Thunderbird. It will do in a pinch though, and will be sufficient for many users.

If you have already signed in to your Windows 8 computer or tablet with a compatible Microsoft account like one from Hotmail.com or Live.com, Mail is already set up and ready to use. You can skip the first few sections that deal with the set-up process. If you have another email account, you'll have to add that manually. Once your email accounts are ready, accessing new mail and composing your own is a simple process.

Access email

If you haven't used Mail yet but you know you logged in to your Windows 8 computer with a Microsoft account you believe to be compatible, open Mail and see if the account is configured. You may be in for a surprise!

1 Locate the Mail icon on the Start screen and click it.

2 If an email account is already configured, you'll see the related inbox and folders. You may even have email!

3 If you see mail there, click once to read it.

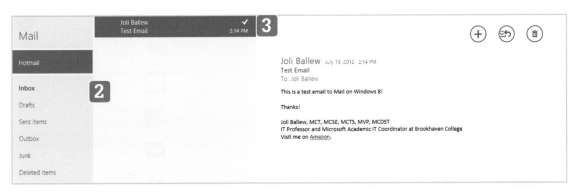

Set up an email account

If you use an email account you obtained from an entity other than Microsoft (such as Gmail), you'll have to set up the account manually. You access the option to add an account from the Settings charm while inside the Mail app.

1 Open Mail and then access the charms. You can use the Windows key + C or flick inwards from the right side of a touch screen. Click Settings.

2 From the Settings options, click Accounts.

3 Click Add an account and then choose the type of accound to add.

4 Fill out the information when prompted, including your email account and password.

5 Click Connect.

6 If you receive an email that requires you to finish setting up your account, follow the directions provided to do so.

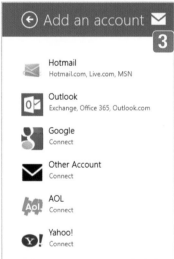

HOT TIP: When you add an email address, it adds your Contacts and Calendar entries associated with the account.

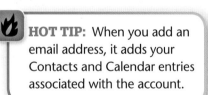 **DID YOU KNOW?**
Mail supports Exchange, Office 365 and Outlook.com email accounts. These are sometimes corporate email accounts.

 HOT TIP: At the website for Gmail, Hotmail, Live Mail and so on, create folders (or labels) for organising email you want to keep. You'll see those folders in the Mail app the next time you log on.

Read email

Mail gets email automatically and without any intervention from you. If you want to check for email manually though, you can click the Sync charm any time you want.

1 If you have more than one email account configured, select the account to use.

2 Right-click the screen or flick upwards to view the charms. Click Sync.

3 Click the email to read.

> ⚠️ **ALERT:** Each email account you configure has its own inbox. Click the Inbox to switch between multiple accounts.

> 🔥 **HOT TIP:** Always delete email immediately after you read it if you don't need to keep it for future reference. This will help keep your inboxes clean and tidy.

WHAT DOES THIS MEAN?

Inbox: This folder holds mail you've received.

Outbox: This folder holds mail you've written but have not yet sent.

Sent items: This folder stores copies of messages you've sent.

Deleted items: This folder holds mail you've deleted.

Drafts: This folder holds messages you've started and saved but not completed. You can save a draft by clicking the X in the email you're composing.

Junk or **Spam:** This folder holds email deemed to be spam. You should check this folder occasionally, since Mail may put email in there that you want to read.

Compose and send a new email

You compose an email message by clicking the + sign in the upper right-hand corner. You input who the email should be sent to and the subject, and then you type the message. If you like, you can click the + sign that is located just to the right of the To line, and choose your recipient(s) from the People app.

1 Click the + sign.

2 Type the recipient's email address in the To line. You can type multiple addresses. Click Show More (not shown).

3 Type a subject in the Subject field.

4 Type the message in the body pane.

5 Click the Send icon.

Reply to or forward an email

When someone sends you an email, you may need to send a reply to them. You do that by selecting the email and then clicking the Reply button. You can forward the email to others using the same technique.

1 Select the email you want to reply to or forward.

2 Click the Reply button. Make the appropriate choice.

3 If desired, change the subject, and then type the message in the body pane.

4 Click Send.

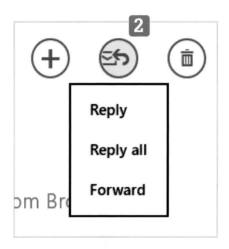

! ALERT: If the email you are replying to was sent to you along with additional people, clicking Reply will send a reply to the person who composed the message. Clicking Reply all will send the reply to everyone who received the email.

HOT TIP: Mail offers formatting tools that you can use to change the font, font colour, font size and more. Right-click while composing an email to access these options.

Print an email

Sometimes you'll need to print an email or its attachment. You access your printer from the Devices charm.

1 Select the email to print.

2 Bring up the default charms (Windows key + C will show these) and click Devices.

3 Select the printer to use.

4 Configure the print options and click Print.

DID YOU KNOW?

If you use a keyboard, the shortcut Ctrl + P will open the Print window. From there, select the printer and configure printer options, then print.

Attach something to an email

Although email that contains only a message serves its purpose quite a bit of the time, often you'll want to send a photograph, a short video, a sound recording, a document or other data. When you want to add something to your message other than text, it's called adding an attachment.

1 Click the + sign to create a new mail message. Select the recipients, type a subject, and compose the email.

2 Right-click or flick upwards to access the charms, then click Attachments.

3 Locate the file to attach and click it.

4 Click Attach (not shown).

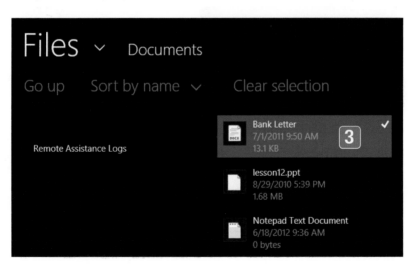

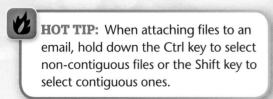 **HOT TIP:** When attaching files to an email, hold down the Ctrl key to select non-contiguous files or the Shift key to select contiguous ones.

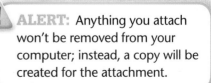 **ALERT:** Anything you attach won't be removed from your computer; instead, a copy will be created for the attachment.

View an attachment in an email

An attachment is a file that you can send with an email, such as a picture, document or video clip. If an email you receive contains an attachment, you'll see a paperclip. To open the attachment, click the paperclip icon in the Preview pane and click the attachment's name.

1 Click the email that contains the attachment.

2 Locate the paperclip icon and click it once.

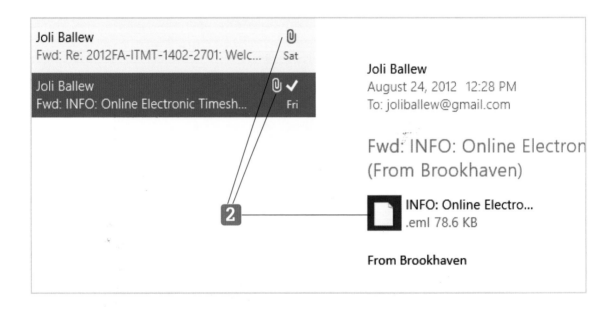

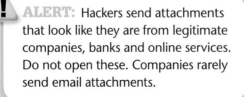

View junk email

Most email accounts have a Junk or Spam folder. If an email is suspected to be spam, it gets sent there. (Spam is another word for junk email.) Unfortunately, sometimes email that is actually legitimate email gets sent to this folder. Therefore, once a week or so you should look in this folder to see whether any email you want to keep is in there.

1 Click once on the junk or spam folder.

2 Use the scroll bars if necessary to browse through the email in the folder.

3 If you see an email that is legitimate, click it once.

4 Right-click to access the charms, and click Move.

5 Click Inbox.

Move **4**

 HOT TIP: If email from a person you know is deemed junk mail but is not, add that person to your contacts.

 ALERT: Mail requires routine maintenance, including deleting email from the junk email folder, among other things. You'll learn how to delete items in a folder next.

Delete email in a folder

In order to keep Mail from getting bogged down, you'll need to delete email often. Depending on how much email you get, this may be as often as once a week.

1 Select any folder that contains mail to delete.

2 Select the mail to delete. (Hold down the Shift key to select multiple email.)

3 Click the Trash icon.

Delete (Ctrl+D)

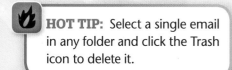 **HOT TIP:** Select a single email in any folder and click the Trash icon to delete it.

ALERT: Don't forget to empty your Sent items folders occasionally too.

Explore formatting options

While composing an email you may want to make text bold, change the colour or font, or perform similar tasks. There are two ways to bring up the editing tools: select any text or right-click. You'll then have access to the following.

- Font – to change the font and font size.
- Bold – to make text bold.
- Italic – to slant the text.
- Underline – to draw a line under text.
- Text Color – to change the colour of selected text.
- Emoticons – to add graphics to an email.
- More – to add bulleted lists, numbered lists, and to undo and redo.

? DID YOU KNOW?

Emoticons are graphics you add to an email to express your feelings when text won't do. You can add smiley faces, sad faces, red lips, broken hearts and so on.

 HOT TIP: When exploring emoticons, click the food icon, the plane icon and others to explore additional categories of graphics

 HOT TIP: Add colour to text in one email to draw attention to it or make a point.

6 View, navigate and share photos

Introduction

Windows 8 comes with several ways to view, navigate and share your photos. One is the Photos app available from the Start screen. From there you can access all of your pictures in a single place, and you can view, print and share them easily. You can also access pictures you've made available online such as those stored in Facebook, Flickr and SkyDrive.

If you'd like to do something a bit more complex, perhaps create folders to organise your photos, rotate them or open them in an editing program, you'll want to do so from the Desktop, specifically using File Explorer. There you can access your Pictures library, move and organise pictures easily, and use the File Explorer interface to share photos in lots of different ways (including burning them to a CD or DVD). You can even sort photos by date, rating, when the pictures were taken, and more.

Navigate photos

The Photos app, available from the Start screen, is the easiest place to view your photos. The app separates your photos by what's stored on your computer, and what is stored in various places on the Internet. If you've created subfolders to organise your photos, those subfolders will appear too.

1 From the Start screen, click Photos.

2 Note the folders that already appear. This is the landing page.

3 Click the Pictures library.

4 If you see subfolders, click them to access the pictures stored there.

HOT TIP: You may not have any photos on your computer yet. If this is the case, skip forward to learn how to import pictures from an external source and then return here to view them.

ALERT: When you save pictures to your computer, make sure you save them to the Pictures library. You can save them specifically to the My Pictures or the Public Pictures folder as well. This will make your pictures easy to find in the Photos app.

View a photo

As you navigate the Photos app, clicking folders and subfolders, you'll see the photos you've stored on your computer. While in folders or subfolders, the photos are in preview mode. You can view them this way or click them to view them in full screen mode. We'll explore both here.

1 Open the Photos app from the Start screen.

2 Click the Pictures library.

3 If applicable, click any subfolder. You'll see photos in Preview mode.

4 Click any photo to view it in full screen mode.

5 Use the back arrow that appears near the middle of the left side of the screen or the one that appears in the top left corner to return to the previous screen.

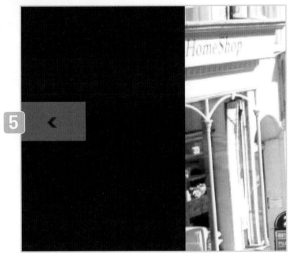

HOT TIP: While in Preview mode, flick or use the scroll wheel on your mouse to move through the photos quickly.

HOT TIP: If you don't see the back arrow, right-click the screen. A secondary back arrow will appear in the top left corner.

Import pictures from an external source

You can put photos on your computer in lots of ways, but the easiest way is to use the Photos app. The landing page offers an option to add a device to *see* photos that are there, but if you right-click while on that page, the option to *import* those photos appears.

1. Connect your camera, insert a memory card or connect an external drive that contains photos.

2. Open the Photos app, and click any back buttons as necessary to access the landing page.

3. Right-click the landing page to access the toolbar.

4. Click Import. If applicable, select the connected device from the options.

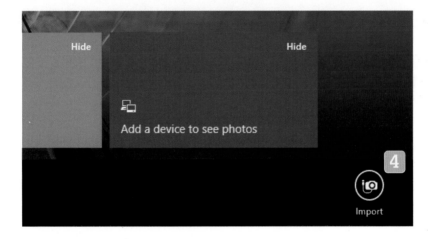

WHAT DOES THIS MEAN?

Import: When you import photos, you copy them to your computer.

5 By default, all of the photos are selected, provided they have not already been imported. Click to deselect photos.

6 Type a name for the folder these pictures will be imported to, and then click Import.

KODAK (E:) 8 files Clear selection

8 files will be imported to this folder

Home Sweet Home **6**   ✕ | Import | Cancel |

6

7 Click Open folder (not shown) to view the photos.

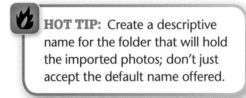

HOT TIP: Create a descriptive name for the folder that will hold the imported photos; don't just accept the default name offered.

Play a slide show of photos

You can play a slide show of pictures in any folder. Once it starts to play, you can stop it in many ways. You can click Esc on the keyboard, right-click with a mouse, touch the screen and more.

1 Open the Photos app from the Start screen.

2 Navigate to any folder that contains photos.

3 Right-click and choose Slide show. (Remember, on a tablet you can swipe up.)

4 Stop the show using any method you prefer.

 HOT TIP: You can pause a slide show by tapping a key on the keyboard, and start it again with a right-click of the mouse (you'll have to click Slide show again).

? DID YOU KNOW?
You won't have any pictures available under SkyDrive, Facebook or Flickr until you click and log in with your account.

Delete photos

You can delete photos that are stored on your own computer from the Photos app. You cannot delete photos that are stored on Facebook and the like. You have to access that website to delete photos stored there.

1 In the Photos app, navigate to a picture stored in your Pictures library folder.

2 Right-click the photo to delete (it can be in preview or full screen mode). In preview mode, a tick will appear on the picture.

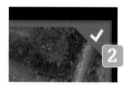

3 If desired, and if you are in preview mode, right-click additional photos.

4 Click Delete.

Clear selection   2 selected   Delete

HOT TIP: If you change your mind about the photos you've selected for deletion, either right-click a single photo to remove the tick (and deselect it), or click Clear selection to clear all selections.

? DID YOU KNOW?

It's best to delete photos you don't want. Unwanted photos not only make the Photos app harder to navigate, the photos also take up valuable hard drive space on your computer.

Use a photo on the Lock screen

You can set a photo to be the background on the Lock screen, the image for an app tile or even serve as an app background.

1 Open the Photos app from the Start screen.

2 Navigate to a photo and open it in full screen.

3 Right-click to access the toolbar, and then click Set as and Lock screen.

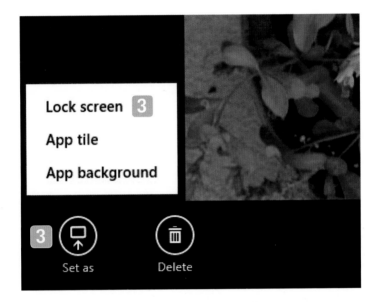

Lock screen 3

App tile

App background

3

Set as   Delete

 HOT TIP: To change the picture that appears on the Photos tile on the Start screen, choose Set as and then App tile.

 HOT TIP: To change the picture that appears on the landing page of the Photos app, choose Set as and then App background.

? **DID YOU KNOW?**
The Photos tile is a live tile, and by default it will flip through photos. From the Start screen, right-click the tile to access the option to disable the live feature.

Connect social accounts

You can view the pictures stored on SkyDrive, Facebook or Flickr from the Photos app. You'll have to click their respective tiles and log in with your account first (if prompted) to use those areas though.

1 From the Photos app, on the landing page, click Facebook or Flickr.

2 Click Connect.

3 If prompted, type your email or user name, and your password.

3 Click Log In (not shown).

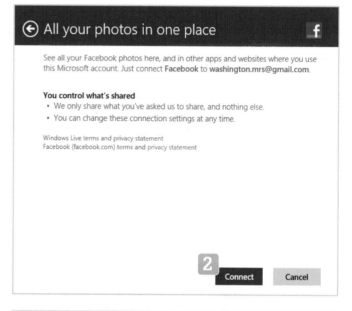

← All your photos in one place   **f**

See all your Facebook photos here, and in other apps and websites where you use this Microsoft account. Just connect **Facebook** to **washington.mrs@gmail.com**.

You control what's shared
- We only share what you've asked us to share, and nothing else.
- You can change these connection settings at any time.

Windows Live terms and privacy statement
Facebook (facebook.com) terms and privacy statement

2 Connect   Cancel

f Facebook Login

Log in to use your Facebook account with Microsoft.

Email:

Password: **3**

☐ Keep me logged in

Forgot your password?

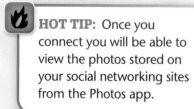

HOT TIP: Once you connect you will be able to view the photos stored on your social networking sites from the Photos app.

? DID YOU KNOW?

If you decide later you don't want to connect to a specific social network from Photos, from the Settings charm, click the Settings option. From there you can hide any previously connected site. (Use the Windows key + C to access the default charms.)

Access your Pictures library on the Desktop

Music, pictures, documents, videos and other data are stored on your computer's hard drive, and are organised in folders and libraries. You can navigate to that data with File Explorer. You will want to do this when you want to perform tasks you can't achieve in the Photos app, such as burning a group of photos to a CD or DVD, among other things.

1 From the Start screen, click Desktop.

2 On the Taskbar, click the folder icon.

3 Double-click Pictures in the content area, or, click Pictures in the Navigation pane.

4 What you see in the resulting window are the pictures available to you from your Pictures library. You may see subfolders you've already created.

? DID YOU KNOW?

From the View tab you can choose how to show the items in a folder. We prefer Large icons, but you can also choose Extra large icons, Medium icons, List, Small icons and others.

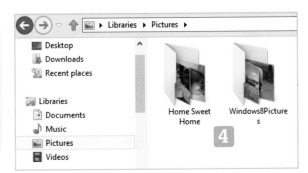

WHAT DOES THIS MEAN?

Library: Offers access to data stored in two related folders. As an example, the Pictures library offers access to the My Pictures folder and the Public Pictures folder.

Explore the File Explorer ribbon

File Explorer has three main features. The Navigation pane is the vertical pane on the left, the Content pane is the larger area on the right, and the ribbon is the area just above both, near the top of the screen. When you select a folder in the Navigation pane and/or content in the Content pane, what appears on the ribbon changes.

1. In File Explorer, click Pictures in the Navigation pane. That's the pane that appears on the left side and contains Favorites, Libraries, Computer, Network and so on.

2. In the Content pane, navigate to a photo and click it once.

3. From the ribbon, click the Share tab. Note a few of the options:
   a. Email – to email a photo. (You'll need to have a compatible email client configured for this to be available.)
   b. Burn to disk – to copy selected photos to a CD or DVD.
   c. Print – to print a photo.

ALERT: If you can't see the Navigation pane, click the View tab. Then click Navigation pane and click Navigation pane from the drop-down list.

ALERT: If the ribbon appears only when you click a tab title, but does not appear all the time, click the down-facing arrow located in the top right corner of the File Explorer window.

4 From the ribbon, click the Home tab. Note a few of the options:

   a. Copy – to copy the photo for pasting elsewhere.

   b. Move to – to move the photo to a different folder.

   c. Delete – to delete the photo.

   d. Rename – to rename the photo.

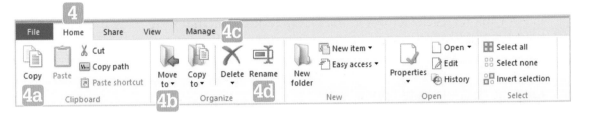

5 From the ribbon, click the Manage tab. Note a few of the options:

   a. Rotate left or Rotate right – to rotate the image.

   b. Slide show – to play a slide show using the images in the folder (or the selected images).

   c. Set as background – to use the selected image(s) as background on the Desktop.

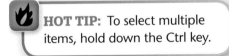 **HOT TIP:** To select multiple items, hold down the Ctrl key.

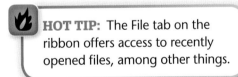 **HOT TIP:** The File tab on the ribbon offers access to recently opened files, among other things.

ALERT: From the View tab, we've selected Large icons. If you have something else selected, what you see will look quite different from what you see here.

Rotate a photo

If you worked through the last section, you can probably figure out how to rotate a photo. For the sake of completeness though, and because photos often need to be rotated, we'll detail it here.

1 Open File Explorer and navigate to a photo that needs to be rotated.

2 Click the photo once.

3 Click the Manage tab.

4 Click the desired rotate option.

View pictures with the Windows Photo Viewer

By default, if you double-click a picture while in File Explorer (in order to view it in full screen mode), the Photos app opens to show it. If you don't want to use the app and would rather view the picture on the Desktop instead, you'll want to opt for Windows Photo Viewer.

1 While in File Explorer, right-click the photo to view.

2 Position your mouse over Open with, and click Windows Photo Viewer.

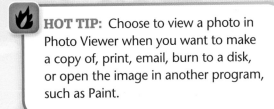

HOT TIP: Choose to view a photo in Photo Viewer when you want to make a copy of, print, email, burn to a disk, or open the image in another program, such as Paint.

3 Note the available options:

   a. File – to delete, make a copy, view the image properties, or exit the program.

   b. Print – to print using your own printer or to order prints online.

   c. E-mail – to email the photo.

   d. Burn – to burn the image to a data disk.

   e. Open – to open the image in another program.

   f. Zoom options – to zoom in and then out of an image.

   g. Previous – to view the previous image in the folder.

   h. Slide Show – to start a slide show of the images in the folder (click Esc to exit).

   i. Next – to view the next image in the folder.

   j. Rotate options – to rotate the photo.

   k. Delete – to delete the photo.

HOT TIP: If you see an additional pane to the right of the Content pane in File Explorer, you can make it go away from the View tab. Click either the Preview pane or Details pane to hide it. (Alternatively, you can opt to show it!)

Print a photo

If you've explored Windows Photo Viewer, you know you can print a photo from there. You can also access the print command from inside File Explorer.

1 Navigate to a single photo to print.

2 Click the photo and then click the Share tab on the ribbon.

3 Click Print.

4 Use the drop-down lists to choose a printer, a paper size, quality settings and paper type.

5 Depending on your selections in step 4, you may also be able to choose how many prints to include on a single page.

6 Configure additional options if applicable and click Print.

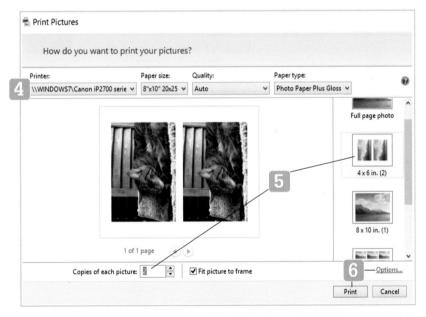

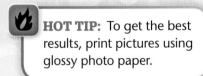

HOT TIP: To get the best results, print pictures using glossy photo paper.

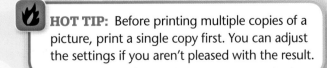

HOT TIP: Before printing multiple copies of a picture, print a single copy first. You can adjust the settings if you aren't pleased with the result.

Email a photo

You can use the Mail app to attach photos to an email you've already started, or you can start an email using File Explorer. When you select photos to email from File Explorer, you're prompted to choose what size to configure the photos. This is a great feature, because it enables you to easily resize the photos however you desire. You'll have to have a dedicated email client though, like Microsoft Office Outlook or something similar.

1 In File Explorer, select the photos to email. (Remember, you can hold down the Ctrl key to select multiple photos.)

2 From the Share tab, click Email. Alternatively, you can right-click any selected photo, and choose Send to>Mail recipient.

3 Use the drop-down list to choose the desired photo size. When sending multiple photos, it's best to keep the total size below 2 MB.

4 Click Attach and complete the email as desired.

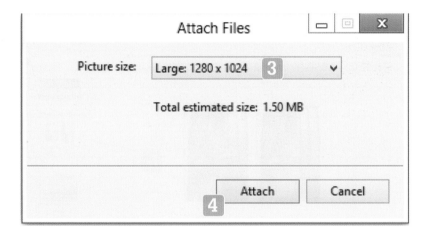

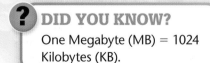

? DID YOU KNOW?
One Megabyte (MB) = 1024 Kilobytes (KB).

! ALERT: You can send videos in an email too, using the same method. Be careful of the size though; videos can be quite large.

Sort photos

The photos that appear in any File Explorer window are sorted automatically by their name. You can sort them differently though, perhaps by size, by the date they were taken, and more.

1 Navigate to any folder that contains photos.

2 Click the View tab.

3 Click Sort by and select a new option.

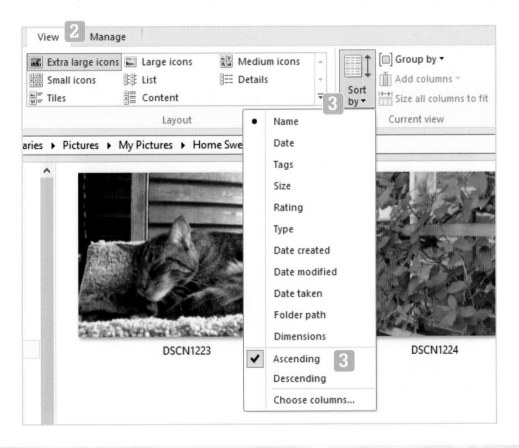

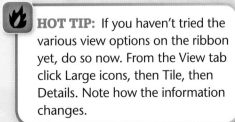

HOT TIP: If you choose to sort by, say, date taken, and the images appear from newest to oldest, you can reverse the order (oldest to newest) by clicking the same option again in the Sort by drop-down list.

HOT TIP: If you haven't tried the various view options on the ribbon yet, do so now. From the View tab click Large icons, then Tile, then Details. Note how the information changes.

Explore editing options

You can edit photos, but you'll need to use an editing program. To find out what your editing options are, right-click any photo while inside File Explorer and choose Edit. Paint may open. Paint is a desktop application included with Windows 8. Paint isn't a very good editing tool though. Consider the following instead.

- Windows Live Photo Gallery – this is part of the free Windows Live Essentials suite. Like most editing programs, it enables you to fix red-eye, crop, adjust exposure and sharpness, and more. There are lots of automatic fixes to make it easy.

- Picasa – this is a free, digital photo *organiser*, so it might complicate locating and managing photos, but the editing tools that come with the program enable you to edit photos quickly and easily. Picasa offers the usual editing tools including crop and various auto adjustments.

- Photoshop Elements – you'll have to pay for this program, but for what you get, it's well worth the cost if you want to do some serious editing. The interface is user friendly, and enables you to edit your photos in ways you never imagined.

HOT TIP: If you have an editing program installed the program may open or you may be prompted regarding which program to use.

HOT TIP: Try Windows Live Photo Gallery first. It's made by Microsoft so you know it will work well with Windows 8.

HOT TIP: Almost all editing programs have an Undo or Revert command. Apply it before you save the file to undo any changes you don't like.

7 View, manage, and listen to music and media

Introduction

You've probably seen the Music and Video apps on the Start screen. These apps are similar to other apps you've explored, including the Store app and the Photos app. Both offer a streamlined interface with limited functionality, making it easy to listen to music and watch videos. It's equally easy to purchase media there too.

When you need to do more than purchase or play media, you can use the desktop app, Windows Media Player. Like other desktop apps you've explored, Media Player offers much more functionality, many more features, and more ways to manage media than either of its app counterparts.

Find your music in the Music app

The Music app, available from the Start screen, offers access to the music you have on your computer. You can use this app to play and control music, and to view information about an artist, among other things.

1 From the Start screen, click the Music tile.

2 If you have music in your Music library, you'll see it under My Music.

3 If you click My Music, you'll have access to all of your music.

4 Click the Back button to return to the Music app's landing page.

? DID YOU KNOW?
If you've obtained audiobooks and saved them to your computer in a compatible file format that the Music app recognizes, you'll see those audiobooks listed in My Music.

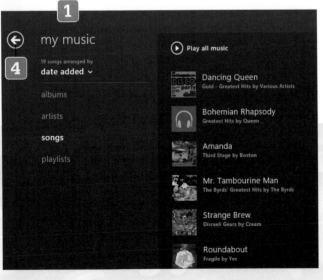

HOT TIP: In My Music, click songs, albums, artist, and playlists to see what's available.

Explore the Music store

If you have a Microsoft account, you can access the Store where you can buy music online. You can also preview the media before you buy it.

1 Open the Music app and click the back arrow as necessary to access the Music app's landing page.

2 Use the scroll bar at the bottom of the screen, the wheel on your mouse, or use your finger to scroll to the right.

3 Click xbox music store to enter the Store.

4 Click a genre in the left pane. A few are shown here.

5 Continue browsing in this manner, and then click an album or song title to see the related details page.

6 Click back buttons as necessary to return to the Music app's landing page.

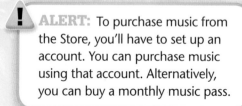

HOT TIP: Use the key combination Windows + I to access the Settings charm. From there you can configure preferences for the Music app.

ALERT: To purchase music from the Store, you'll have to set up an account. You can purchase music using that account. Alternatively, you can buy a monthly music pass.

Play a song or listen to an audiobook

If you have music in your Music library you can play it from the Music app. If you don't have any music, you can copy songs from CDs you own. You'll learn how to do that later in this chapter.

1 Open the Music app and navigate to any album (or song or audiobook) to play.

2 Click it to access the details page. Click any song.

3 Click Play or Play album, or make any other choice.

4 Explore the playback options at the bottom of the screen. You may have to flick up or right-click to access these.

5 Click the album cover, located in the middle of the toolbar, to view the album cover, track list, artist information, and more.

HOT TIP: You can play an entire album by clicking Play album in the left pane of the available Details page.

DID YOU KNOW?
As you add music to your Music library, the songs and albums will appear in the Music app automatically.

Navigate the Video app and watch a video

The Video app is very similar to the Music app. It contains a My Videos section, and offers access to the Store, where you can purchase movies and TV shows. If you have video, perhaps something you've purchased or something you've taken yourself with a video camera, you'll probably see it here.

1 From the Start screen, open the Video app.

2 If you have video in your Video library, you'll see it under My Videos.

3 Use the scroll bar, the scroll wheel on your mouse, or flick with your finger to see the other video options, including options to purchase media.

4 To play a video, click it one time.

5 The video will play and controls will become available on the screen.

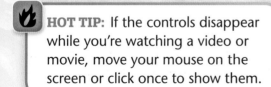

HOT TIP: If the controls disappear while you're watching a video or movie, move your mouse on the screen or click once to show them.

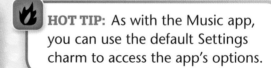

HOT TIP: As with the Music app, you can use the default Settings charm to access the app's options.

Explore Media Player

Windows Media Player is a desktop app. You open Media Player the same way you open other programs, from the Start screen. Just type *media* and select Windows Media Player from the results. Once opened, you'll need to know where the Library button is so that you can access different kinds of media.

1 Open Windows Media Player.

2 Click the arrow next to the Library button.

3 Click Music. (Music may already be selected.) Note the other options.

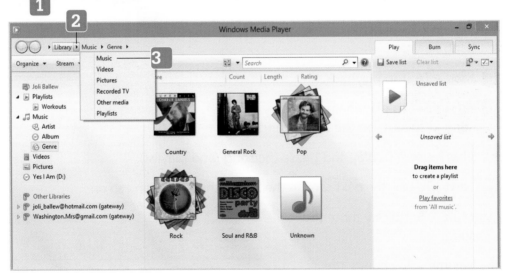

Play a song in Media Player

To play any song, navigate to it and double-click it. Once the song is playing you can manage the media using the playback controls located at the bottom of the Media Player interface.

1. Open Media Player, and click Music in the Navigation pane. (Note you can also click Artist, Album, or Genre to locate a song.)

2. Double-click any song to play it.

Use these media controls located at the bottom of the Media Player interface:

3. Shuffle – To let Windows Media Player choose what order to play the selected songs.

4. Repeat – To play the current song again.

5. Stop – To stop playback.

6. Previous – To play the previous song in the list, on the album, and so on.

7. Play/Pause – To play and pause the song (and playlist).

8. Next – To play the next song in the list, on the album, and so on.

9. Mute – To quickly mute the song.

10. Volume – To change the volume of the song.

HOT TIP: While a song is playing, right-click any other song and choose Play Next, Play All, or Play, as desired.

? DID YOU KNOW?
Media Player has Back and Forward buttons you can use to navigate it.

Copy a CD to your computer

You can copy your own music CDs to your hard drive. This is called 'ripping'. To rip means to copy in media-speak. Once music is on your PC, you can listen to it in the Music app and in Media Player, burn compilations of music to other CDs, and sync the music to a portable music player.

1 Insert the CD to copy into the CD drive.

2 Deselect any songs you do not want to copy to your PC.

3 In Windows Media Player, click the Rip CD button.

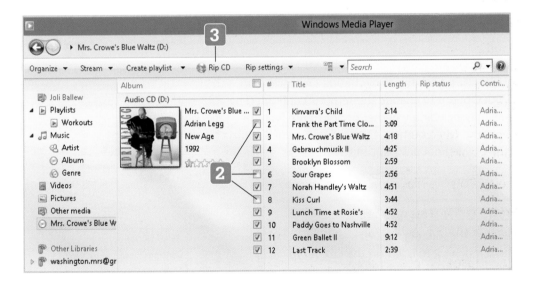

 HOT TIP: Right-click any album cover and click Find Album Info, and Windows Media Player will look online for the album cover, track list, and other information.

? DID YOU KNOW?
You have the right to rip any CD you own to your PC for no extra cost and without breaking any laws.

HOT TIP: Click the arrow beside Organize, and click Options to change the settings configured by default, such as what format you use when you rip a CD. (You'll want to choose MP3 if you plan to copy the music to a portable player, for instance.)

Copy music files to a CD

There are two ways to take music with you when you are on the road or on the go. You can copy the music to a portable device (music player, tablet, or phone) or you can create your own CDs, choosing the songs to copy and placing them on the CD in the desired order.

1 Open Media Player.

2 Insert a blank CD and click the Burn tab.

3 Click any song or album to add and drag it to the List pane, shown here. You can drag any song to move it to a new position in the burn list.

4 When you've added the songs you want, click Start burn.

HOT TIP: Click the arrow beside Organize, and click Options to change the settings configured by default, including whether or not to use 'volume leveling' when burning CDs or if you want to burn the CD without any gaps between tracks.

? DID YOU KNOW?
Look at the slider in the List pane to see how much room is left on the CD. A typical CD can hold about 80 minutes of music.

WHAT DOES THIS MEAN?
Burn: a term used to describe the process of copying music from a computer to a CD.

8 Stay in touch with others

Introduction

Windows 8 offers two apps to help you keep in touch with your contacts. One is Messaging, the other, People. Messaging lets you chat via text with friends who use various messaging services including Facebook and Windows Messenger, and offers app commands on a toolbar that let you invite others and delete conversations. The People app holds the contact information you keep about others, and offers access to your friends' social networking updates. Like Messaging, there are commands that enable you to configure the app to suit your preferences.

Navigate Messaging

The first time you open the Messaging app, you'll be greeted with a message from the Windows Messaging team. You can't reply to this message, but it does give you a sense of how you'll use the app in the future.

1 From the Start screen, click the Messaging tile to open it.

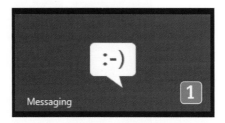

2 Right-click or flick upwards from the bottom with your finger to see the available charms.

3 Note the options to change your status, invite others and delete a conversation.

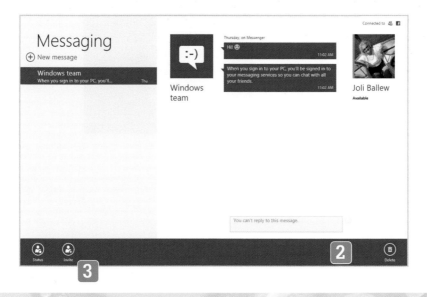

4 Use the Windows key + C keyboard shortcut to bring up the charms. Click the Settings charm.

5 Note the options. You can add accounts, configure options, view permissions and more.

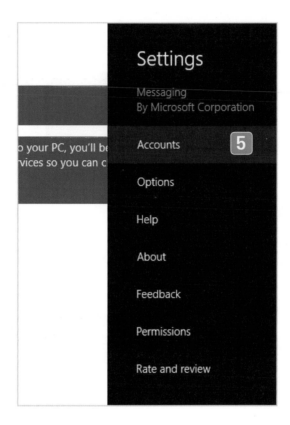

? DID YOU KNOW?

If you click the option to invite people from the toolbar, you'll have to choose from where to invite them, give permission for Microsoft to access the chosen accounts and so on.

 HOT TIP: You can't send traditional text and SMS messages to mobile phones and smartphones from the Messaging app.

Add social networking information

You add social networking information such as your Facebook user name and password so that you can communicate with others who also use that service and are your contacts there.

1. While inside the Messaging app, access the default charms (Windows key + C or flick inwards from the right side of the screen).

2. Click the Settings charm and then click Accounts.

3. Click Add an account.

4. Choose the account from the resulting list.

5. Click Connect and input the required information.

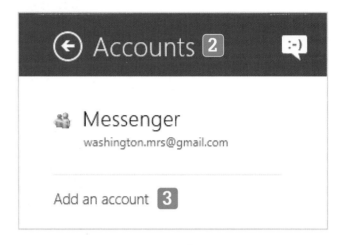

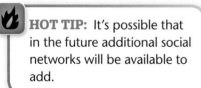

HOT TIP: It's possible that in the future additional social networks will be available to add.

DID YOU KNOW?
You can't send a message to a Facebook friend if they aren't online.

Invite a friend

You can start a new conversation with any contact who is online that is also saved in the People app. You may not have every contact there though so you can use the Invite option to add a contact when this is the case.

1 Right-click or flick upwards from the bottom (or down from the top) to access the toolbar.

2 Click Invite and then Add a new friend.

3 To add a single contact using their email address, type that address and click Next; click Invite.

4 When the contact accepts your invitation, you'll be able to chat with them via Messaging.

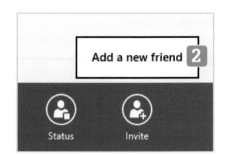

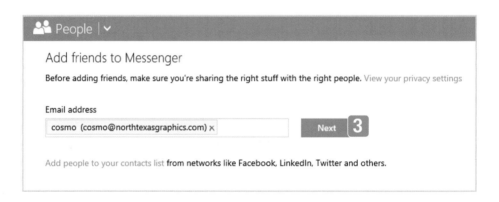

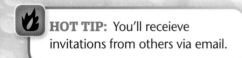

HOT TIP: You'll receieve invitations from others via email.

? DID YOU KNOW?
You can choose to invite people from other services instead of adding a single contact. What you have to do to complete this task depends on your selection.

Write a message

To start a new conversation with someone (also called a 'thread'), click the New message option in the Messaging app.

1 In the Messaging app, click New Message.

2 The People app will open. Choose the desired contact and click Choose.

3 Type your message in the text message window and press Enter. Your message will appear at the top of the page.

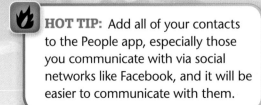
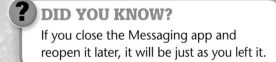

🔥 **HOT TIP:** Add all of your contacts to the People app, especially those you communicate with via social networks like Facebook, and it will be easier to communicate with them.

❓ **DID YOU KNOW?**
If you close the Messaging app and reopen it later, it will be just as you left it.

Respond to a message

Before you can respond to a message you receive, you must first select the contact in the left pane of the Messaging app. (If you have only one conversation going, you won't have to do this.) Once you've selected who to respond to, you simply type your response and press Enter.

1 In the left pane of the Messaging app, select the thread to respond to.

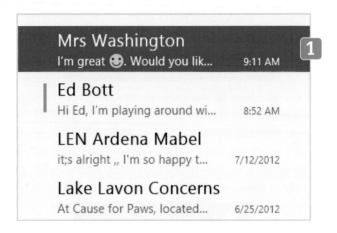

2 Type your message and press Enter on the keyboard.

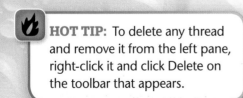 **HOT TIP:** To delete any thread and remove it from the left pane, right-click it and click Delete on the toolbar that appears.

? DID YOU KNOW?
You can change your status from Available to Invisible so people can't communicate with you via Messaging.

Navigate People

You use the People app to organise and make available information about your contacts. Many contacts will automatically appear as you add social networking sites and log on with your own Microsoft account. What you see depends on how you've used your Windows 8 computer so far.

1 Open the People app from the Start screen.

2 Note these options:

   a. Social – to view notifications, your own profiles, update your own status and so on.

   b. What's new – to view status updates, tweets and other social networking data.

   c. Favorites or All – to access your contacts and view information about them.

People **1**

⊕ **Arts Magnet Years**

Contact

Send message
Facebook

Map address
Dallas   **2c**

View profile
Facebook

Facebook

HOT TIP: If you navigate away from the People landing page and can't get back, right-click or flick upwards and click Home to return to it.

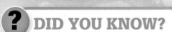 **DID YOU KNOW?**
You can add a contact from the People app from scratch. Right-click or flick upwards and click New to get started.

 HOT TIP: While in the People app, right-click or flick upwards to access the option to filter contacts to show only those that are online. You can probably send those online contacts messages using the Messaging app.

Add a contact manually

It's highly likely that your contacts already appear in the People app. That's because when you connect Windows 8 with your Microsoft account, your Facebook account, your Twitter account and others, contacts are populated automatically. You may want to add a contact manually though, and you can.

1 Open the People app.

2 Right-click or flick upwards to access the toolbar, and click New.

3 Type the desired information. Click any + sign to change the field name.

4 Click Save (not shown).

HOT TIP: To edit a contact after you've saved it, click the contact, right-click or flick upwards to access the Edit option (note the option to pin the contact to the Start screen too), and input the information as desired.

? DID YOU KNOW?
You can delete a contact in the same manner you edit one. Just click Delete on the toolbar.

Add social network user information

Like the Messaging app, you can add information about the social networks you belong to while inside the People app. When you do, you can see their status updates, access their contact information, send them email and messages, and more.

1 While inside the People app, access the default charms (Windows key + C or flick inwards).

2 Click the Settings charm and then click Accounts.

2 Settings

People
By Microsoft Corporation

2 Accounts

Options

Help

About

Feedback

Permissions

Rate and review

? DID YOU KNOW?

If you position your mouse in the bottom right corner of the People app and click the – sign that appears, the screen will change from the large tiles you currently see for your contacts to small, alphabetic tiles you can use to go directly to that group of contacts.

3 Click Add an account.

4 Choose the account from the resulting list.

5 Input the required information and click Connect.

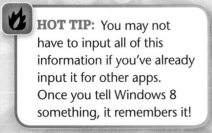

HOT TIP: You may not have to input all of this information if you've already input it for other apps. Once you tell Windows 8 something, it remembers it!

Update your status

You can update your Facebook status or compose a tweet from inside the People app. You'll find the option from the Social area of the app.

1 Open the People app and click Me.

2 Click the arrow available from the What's new section (as applicable).

3 Select Facebook, Twitter, or another available option.

4 Type to update your status or tweet as applicable.

HOT TIP: You can 'like' and comment on Facebook posts, and retweet and reply to Twitter entries from inside the People app.

View others' updates

You view other people's updates, posts and tweets from the What's new option. You can click any option available under an entry to reply, like or respond to it, as applicable. If you have signed in with multiple social networks, you can filter what you see from the toolbar.

1 Open the People app and click What's new.

2 Use your finger to flick left and right, or use the scroll wheel on your mouse to move through the posts. (There's a scroll bar at the bottom of the screen as well.)

3 Notice the options under each post or tweet. Click to respond as desired.

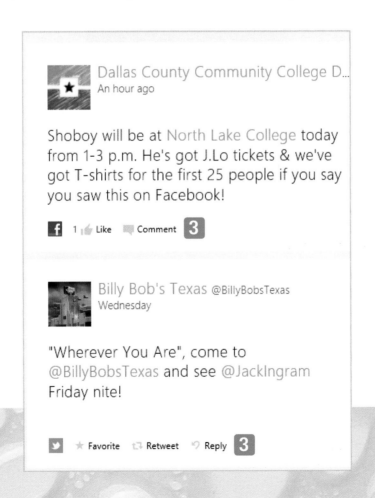

4 Right-click or flick upwards and click Filter.

5 Choose which social network(s) you'd like to view.

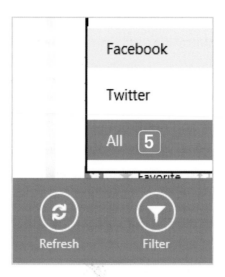

? DID YOU KNOW?

The Refresh button, available next to Filter on the People toolbar, will refresh the information shown under What's new.

HOT TIP: To filter your contacts list by certain social networks, from the Settings charm click Options.

Add shortcuts on the Start screen

If the People app doesn't meet your needs, you can create a shortcut on the Start screen for your favourite social networking websites. You might create shortcuts for Facebook.com, Twitter.com, Live.com, AOL.com, Wordpress.com and so on.

1 From the Start screen, open the Internet Explorer app.

2 Navigate to the website you'd like to create a shortcut for.

3 On the Address bar at the bottom of the page, click the thumbtack and click Pin to Start.

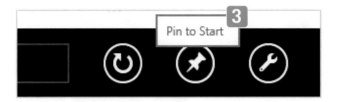

4 Type the desired name and click Pin to Start again.

5 Return to the Start screen, and scroll right. You'll see the new tile there.

? **DID YOU KNOW?**

When you create a shortcut to a website, when you click the tile the full website opens. You might prefer the full website to the People app; if so, add tiles for all of the social networks you use.

Get more social networking apps

You can get more social networking apps from the Store, available from the Start screen, and most are free. You might prefer these apps over what's available now, specifically the Messaging app and the People app.

1 From the Start screen, click Store.

2 Scroll to locate the Social apps.

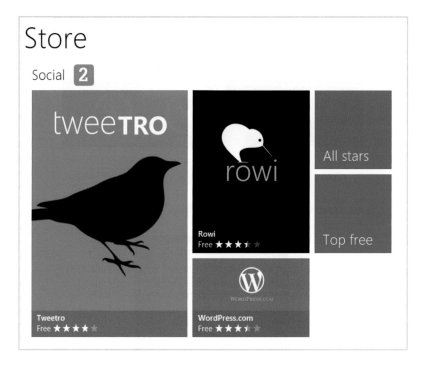

HOT TIP: Make sure to read the reviews before you commit to purchasing an app!

3 Click Top free, New releases, or if the app appears on the screen already, click it.

4 If you like the app after reading the reviews and other information, click Install.

5 Open the app, log in, and repeat!

 HOT TIP: Once you own an app you can review and rate it. You'll see that option on the app page in the Store.

 DID YOU KNOW? You can uninstall any app you don't like from the Start screen's toolbar.

9 Install hardware and software

Introduction

A new PC doesn't often come with everything you need. Most of the time it does not come with a preinstalled printer or scanner, and often you later buy gadgets such as digital cameras or headphones. You may also want to sync and back up smartphones you've purchased. This hardware, as it's referred to, must be installed before it can be used.

Beyond hardware, you'll probably need to install software. Software, in this sense, consists of desktop applications you purchase, such as Microsoft Office or Photoshop Elements, or something you download from the Internet, like iTunes. (We're not talking about installing apps from the Store here.) In this chapter, you'll learn how to install both hardware and software.

Install a digital camera, webcam or smartphone

Most of the time, installing hardware is easy. You simply plug in the device and wait for it to be automatically installed. Once it's installed, you can set what you'd like to happen by default. Before you start, make sure the device is charged, plugged in to a wall outlet or has fresh batteries.

1 Read the directions that came with the device. If there are specific instructions for installing it, follow them. If not, continue here.

2 Connect the device.

3 If applicable, turn on the device. (You may have to set an older digital camera or camcorder to its playback position.)

4 Wait while the driver is installed. When prompted, click or tap to choose what happens when you connect the device next time.

Apple iPhone
Tap to choose what happens with this device. **4**

 HOT TIP: If you missed the prompt to configure what to do when you connect the device and it's no longer available, don't worry. Just diskonnect and reconnect it. It will appear again (at least until you set what you'd like to do all the time).

5 Choose what to do when you connect the device.

Apple iPhone
5
Choose what to do with this device.

 Import photos and videos
Photos

 Open device to view files
Windows Explorer

 Take no action

WHAT DOES THIS MEAN?

Driver: Software that allows the PC and the new hardware to communicate with each other.

Software: A program that may or may not be required for the hardware to function correctly.

USB: A technology used to connect hardware to a PC. A USB cable is often used to connect devices to a PC.

FireWire: A technology used to connect hardware to a PC. A FireWire cable is often used to connect a digital video camera to a PC.

? DID YOU KNOW?

Sometimes you receive a CD with a device. The hardware may work fine without it. If you want to keep unnecessary data and programs off of your PC, see if the hardware will work without it first. You can always install the CD later if you need to.

Install hardware that has a CD

Printers, fax machines and scanners often come with a CD and sometimes features won't be available until you install the software on it. Be careful what you choose to install though; you probably don't need everything that's available.

1 Connect the device to a wall outlet if applicable.

2 Connect the device to the PC using the applicable cable.

3 Insert the CD for the device if you have it.

4 Click the resulting prompt and opt to run the installation file.

5 Work through the set-up process.

6 From the Start screen, type Devices, then Settings. Look for Devices in the results.

7 Click Devices and view the newly installed printer.

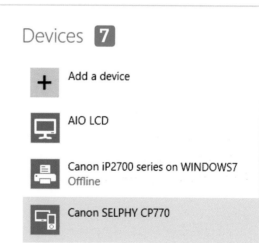

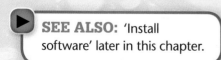

ALERT: Scanners often require specialised software to function. Printers often require specialised software to offer advanced features, such as printing envelopes or both sides of a page.

SEE ALSO: 'Install software' later in this chapter.

ALERT: Read the directions that come with each new device you acquire. If there are specific instructions for installation, follow those directions, not the generic directions offered here.

Add a device manually

If, when you connect and turn on a device, nothing happens, you'll have to install the device manually. Although there is more than one way to add a device in Windows 8, the most comprehensive is to use the Devices and Printers window.

1 Open Control Panel.

2 Under Hardware and Sound, click Add a device. (Note the option View devices and printers; you'll access this later.)

3 If you see the device in the resulting list, select it and click Next. If you do not see the device in the list, proceed to the next section ('Locate a driver').

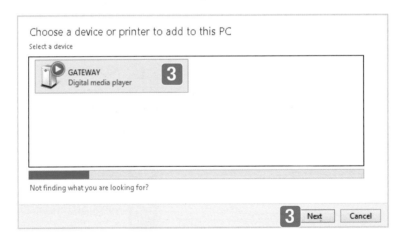

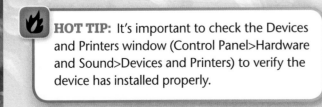

HOT TIP: It's important to check the Devices and Printers window (Control Panel>Hardware and Sound>Devices and Printers) to verify the device has installed properly.

4 Return to the Control Panel, and click View devices and printers. If there is an exclamation mark in the Devices and Printers window beside the device, it's not working properly. Proceed to the next section ('Locate a driver').

? DID YOU KNOW?

Although you can add a device from the PC Settings window from the Devices tab, if there's a problem you'll end up at Control Panel anyway. So it's best just to start there.

? DID YOU KNOW?

You can right-click a device in the Devices and Printers window and click Troubleshoot.

Locate a driver

As noted, most of the time hardware installs automatically and with no input from you (other than plugging it in and turning it on). However, in rare cases, the hardware does not install properly or is simply not available, even if you try to install it manually. If this happens, you'll have to locate and install the driver yourself.

1 Write down the name and model number of the device.

2 Open the Internet Explorer Desktop app and locate the manufacturer's website.

3 Locate a link for Support, Support and Drivers, Customer Support or something similar. Click it.

4 Locate your device driver by make, model or other characteristics.

ZR70MC **4**

▸ Service & Support
▸ Drivers & Software
▸ Brochures & Manuals
▸ Supplies & Accessories

5 Proceed to the next section, 'Download and install a driver'.

 HOT TIP: To find the manufacturer's website, try putting a www. before the company name and a .com after. (www.epson.com, www.hewlett-packard.com and www.apple.com are examples.)

! ALERT: Locating a driver is the first step. You must now download the driver and, later, install it.

 **HOT TIP:** The make and model of a device are probably located on the bottom or back of the device.

Download and install a driver

If you've located the driver you need, you can now download and install it. Downloading is the process of saving the driver to your computer's hard drive. Once downloaded, you can install the driver.

1 Locate the driver as detailed in the previous section. You may have to work through a few more screens to actually get to the driver, such as choosing an operating system or agreeing to terms of service.

2 Click Download Driver, Obtain Software or something similar.

3 Click Save.

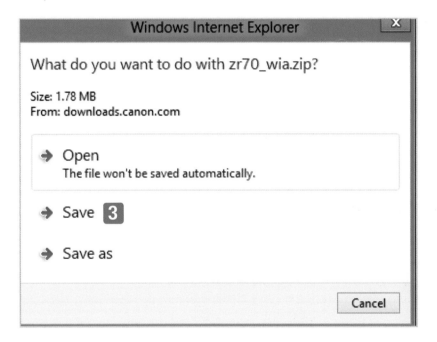

4 Click Open Folder. You'll see this at the bottom of the Internet Explorer Desktop app's window.

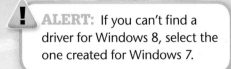 **ALERT:** If you can't find a driver for Windows 8, select the one created for Windows 7.

HOT TIP: Once set-up completes, look again in the Devices and Printers window to verify the hardware has installed properly.

5 As applicable, open a subfolder and look for the Setup or Installation file. It will be an application or executable file.

~~ISSCRIPT~~	~~Windows Installer Packag~~
LICENSE_E_AMERICA	Text Document
LICENSE_E_ASIA	Text Document
LICENSE_E_EUROPE	Text Document
LICENSE_E_OCEANIA	Text Document
README	Text Document
☑ SETUP **5**	Application
SETUP	Configuration settings

6 Double-click the set-up file and work through the set-up process as prompted.

! **ALERT:** If installation does not begin automatically, browse to the location of the file and double-click it to begin the installation manually. You may have to browse to the Downloads folder.

WHAT DOES THIS MEAN?
Executable file: Used to install an application, program or device driver, for example.

Use ReadyBoost

ReadyBoost is a technology that enables you to use a USB flash drive or a secure digital memory card as cache (a place where data is stored temporarily and accessed when needed) to increase computer performance. Cache works like RAM, and more is certainly better!

1 Insert a USB flash drive, thumb drive or memory card into an available slot on the outside of your PC.

2 When prompted in the upper right corner, click to view your options.

3 Choose Speed up my system, Windows ReadyBoost.

4 Choose to dedicate the device to ReadyBoost and click OK.

ALERT: USB keys must be at least USB 2.0 and meet other requirements, but don't worry about that, you'll be told if the hardware isn't up to par.

HOT TIP: Only newer and larger USB keys will work for ReadyBoost.

WHAT DOES THIS MEAN?

RAM: Random access memory is where information is stored temporarily so the operating system has quick access to it. The more RAM you have, the better your PC should perform.

Cache: A temporary storage area similar to RAM.

Install software

As with installing hardware, software installation goes smoothly almost every time. Just make sure you get your software from a reliable source, like Amazon, Microsoft's website, Apple's website (think iTunes, not software for Macs only) or a retail store.

1 Download the installation file from the Internet and skip to step 4, or insert the CD or DVD in the appropriate drive and proceed to step 2.

2 Click the prompt that appears in the top right corner to see your options.

3 If you are not prompted or you miss the prompt:

  a. Open the Computer window. (You can type Computer at the Start screen.)

  b. Double-click the CD or DVD drive.

4 Double-click the application file or do whatever else is necessary to start the installation.

5 Work through the installation wizard.

HOT TIP: If you download software from the Internet, copy the installation files to a CD or DVD for safe keeping and write the product ID or key on it.

ALERT: To install software you must locate the application file or the executable file. Often this is named Setup, Install or something similar. If you receive a message that the file you are trying to open can't be opened, you've chosen the wrong file.

Use Program Compatibility Mode

If you install a software program but it doesn't work properly, you can run it in Program Compatibility Mode. This lets you run programs made for previous versions of Windows. Often this resolves software problems.

1 From the Start screen, type Program Compatibility.

2 Click Settings.

3 Click Run programs made for previous versions of Windows.

4 Click Next to begin.

5 Choose the problematic program. Click Next.

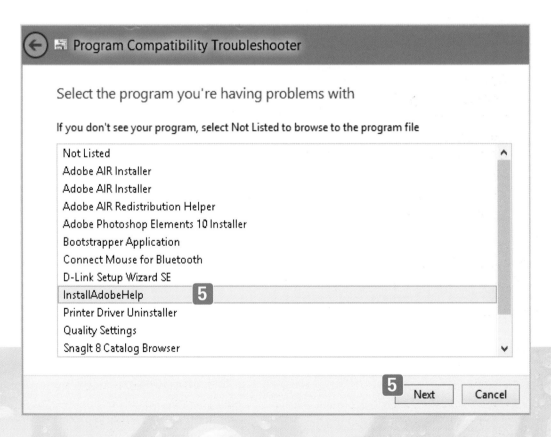

6 Click Troubleshoot problems.

7 Answer the questions as prompted.

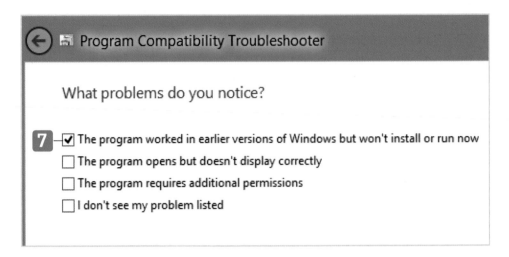

Program Compatibility Troubleshooter

What problems do you notice?

7 — ☑ The program worked in earlier versions of Windows but won't install or run now

☐ The program opens but doesn't display correctly

☐ The program requires additional permissions

☐ I don't see my problem listed

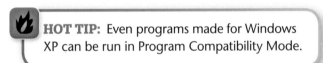

HOT TIP: Even programs made for Windows XP can be run in Program Compatibility Mode.

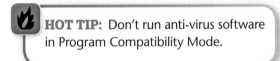

HOT TIP: Don't run anti-virus software in Program Compatibility Mode.

Resolve problems with Action Center

If you've encountered problems that you can't resolve, have no fear. Windows 8 is working in the background to find solutions for you. You can check to see if any suitable solutions have been found in the Action Center.

1 Access the Desktop.

2 On the Taskbar in the Notification Center, click the flag icon.

3 Click Open Action Center.

4 If you see issues in Action Center, such as not having anti-virus software installed, resolve those issues.

5 Click the arrow beside Maintenance.

6 Click Check for solutions.

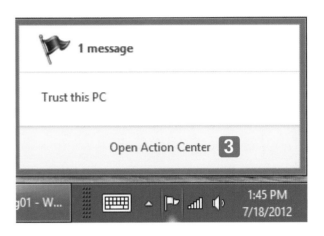

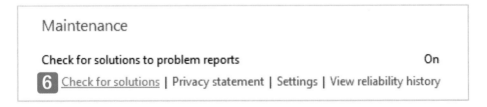

7 If solutions are found, follow the prompts to resolve them.

! ALERT: You have to submit problem reports when prompted for Windows 8 to look for solutions!

? DID YOU KNOW?

The Action Center offers troubleshooting wizards to help you resolve problems related to program installation, hardware, connecting to your network or the Internet, and system and security.

10 Use Desktop applications

Introduction

Desktop applications open on the Desktop, the traditional computing environment (as opposed to the newer Start screen apps that open in their own window, offer their own toolbars and charms, and do not require the Desktop to function). These applications can be programs you install, like Adobe Photoshop Elements or Windows Media Player, or less complex applications that come with new printers, cameras or scanners. They can be Windows Accessories too, like the Calculator, Notepad, the Snipping Tool and Sound Recorder. You have learned already that Windows Media Player is a Desktop application, and you know that Control Panel opens on the Desktop too, as does File Explorer. There are lots of programs that need access to the Desktop to run.

In this chapter you'll learn how to locate the Desktop apps from the Start screen, and how to use a few of them. After that, any time an application opens on the Desktop, you'll understand how to use it and why it's a Desktop app.

Search for a program from the Start screen

The Start screen offers access to the applications, programs, accessories and features available on your computer, including the Desktop apps. If they aren't available on the Start screen itself, look at the All apps screen instead.

1 Access the Start screen. You can press the Windows key to get there.

2 Scroll through what's shown. For the most part, what you see as blue squares are Desktop apps (or features, folders or something similar).

? DID YOU KNOW?

An app is a Desktop app if it opens on the Desktop.

3 Right-click and click All apps.

4 Scroll right and look for additional Desktop apps. A few are shown here.

Notepad	WordPad	Control Panel
Paint	XPS Viewer	Default Programs
Remote Desktop Connection	Windows Ease of Access	File Explorer
Snipping Tool	Magnifier	Help and Support
Sound Recorder	Narrator	Run
Steps Recorder	On-Screen Keyboard	Task Manager
Sticky Notes	Windows Speech Recognition	Windows Defender
Windows Fax and Scan	Windows System	Windows Easy Transfer
Windows Journal	Command Prompt	Windows Easy Transfer Reports

WHAT DOES THIS MEAN?

Desktop: The traditional computing environment and offers the Taskbar, the Recycle Bin icon, the Notification area and so on.

Write a letter with Notepad

If you need to create and print a simple document like a grocery or to-do list, or need to put together a weekly newsletter that you send via email, there's no reason to purchase a large office suite like Microsoft Office (and learn how to use it) when Notepad will do just fine. Although you can't create and insert tables, add endnotes, add text boxes or perform similar tasks with Notepad, you may never need to anyway.

1 From the Start screen, press the Windows key + C to bring up the charms.

2 Click Search.

3 Type Notepad, and then click Notepad. (The Desktop appears with Notepad on it.)

4 Click once inside Notepad, and start typing.

! ALERT: If you close Notepad before saving the file, your work will be lost!

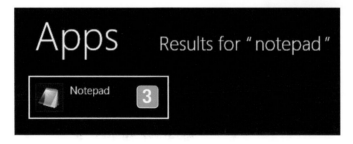

! ALERT: Notepad has five menus: File, Edit, Format, View and Help. After you become familiar with these menus, what you learn will carry over to almost any other program you'll use.

? DID YOU KNOW?
The Format menu includes options for setting the font, font style, font size and more.

Save a letter with Notepad

If you want to save a letter you've written in Notepad so you can work with it later, you have to click File and then click Save (or Save As). This will allow you to name the file and save it to your hard drive. The next time you want to view the file, you can click File and then click Open if Notepad is already open, or you can look for the file from the Start screen by searching for the file name.

1 With Notepad open and a few words typed, click File.

2 Click Save.

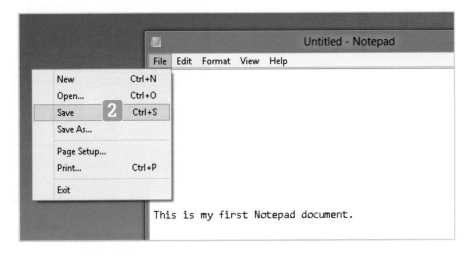

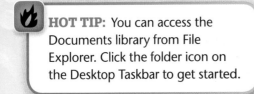

HOT TIP: You can access the Documents library from File Explorer. Click the folder icon on the Desktop Taskbar to get started.

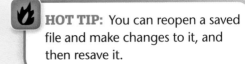

HOT TIP: You can reopen a saved file and make changes to it, and then resave it.

3 Type a unique name for the file. Notice that the default folder for saving a Notepad document is the Documents library.

4 Click Save.

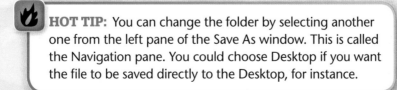

HOT TIP: You can change the folder by selecting another one from the left pane of the Save As window. This is called the Navigation pane. You could choose Desktop if you want the file to be saved directly to the Desktop, for instance.

Print a letter with Notepad

Sometimes you'll need to print a letter so you can post it, print a grocery list to take on a shopping trip, or print a list of steps to complete a task. You can access the Print command from Notepad's File menu. If Notepad isn't open, from the Windows 8 Start screen, type the name of the file, and from the Search pane click Files. Then, click the file in the resulting list.

1 With the document open in Notepad, click File.

2 Click Print.

3 Select a printer (if more than one exists).

4 Set preferences as desired.

5 Click Print.

HOT TIP: You have to have a printer installed, plugged in and turned on to print. Additionally, the Print dialogue box must show that the printer is 'Ready' before you can print to it.

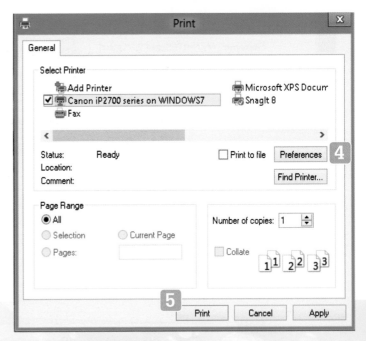

WHAT DOES THIS MEAN?

Printer Preferences: Lets you select the page orientation, print order and the type of paper you'll be printing on, among other features.

Page range: Lets you select what pages to print.

Use the calculator

You've probably used a calculator before, and using the Windows 8 calculator is not much different from a hand-held one, except that you input numbers with a mouse click, keyboard, a number pad, or your finger. There are four calculators available, and Standard is the default. Calculator is available from the All apps screen.

1 From the Start screen, right-click and then click All apps.

2 Scroll right, and under Windows Accessories, click Calculator.

3 Input numbers and operations using any applicable method.

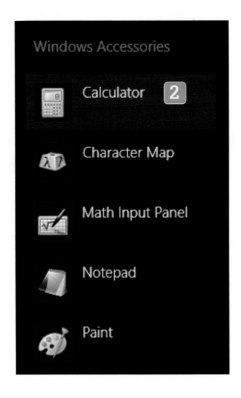

 HOT TIP: If you have trouble using the mouse to click the numbers on the calculator, use the keypad on your keyboard.

4 Click the View menu to see other calculator options. This is the Scientific calculator. Note the other options.

5 Close Calculator by clicking the X in the top right corner.

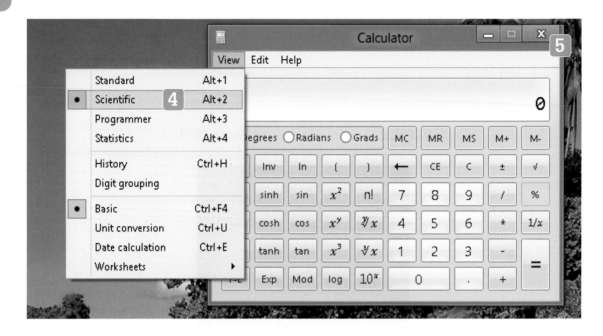

HOT TIP: Explore each menu option and the available features there. Make sure to look at View>Worksheets>Mortgage, to see how worksheets function.

Take a screenshot

Sometimes you'll see something on your screen you want to capture to keep or share. It may be part of a webpage (like a picture of a great pair of shoes or a new car), or an error message you want to share with a technician. The Snipping Tool lets you capture the shot. To use the Snipping Tool, you drag your mouse cursor around any area on the screen to copy and capture it. Once captured, you can save it, edit it and/or send it to an email recipient.

1 From the Start screen, type Snip.

2 In the results, click Snipping Tool.

3 Click New.

HOT TIP: Editing tools will become available after creating a snip. You can write on a clip with a red, blue, black or customised pen or a highlighter, and if you mess up, you can use the eraser.

4 Drag your mouse across any part of the screen. When you let go of the mouse, the snip will appear in the Snipping Tool window.

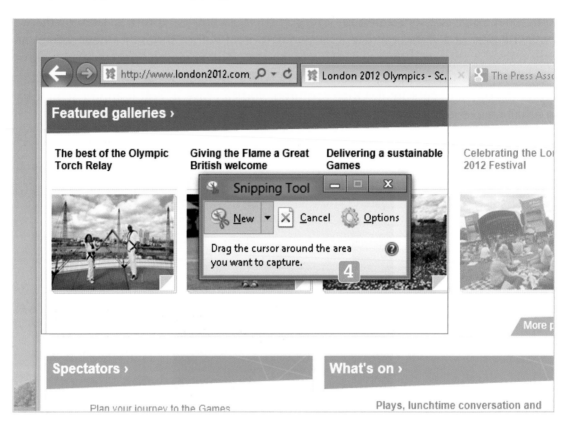

5 Explore each menu: File, Edit, Tools and Help, and the options on the toolbar. Refer to the next task for more information.

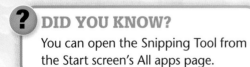

? DID YOU KNOW?

You can open the Snipping Tool from the Start screen's All apps page.

Email a screenshot

You can use the Snipping Tool to take a picture of your screen as detailed in the previous section. You can even write on it with a 'pen'. You can also email that screenshot if you'd like to share it with someone, but you'll need a dedicated email client to do so.

1 Take a screenshot with the Snipping Tool.

2 If desired, use the pen, highlighter and other tools to write on the image.

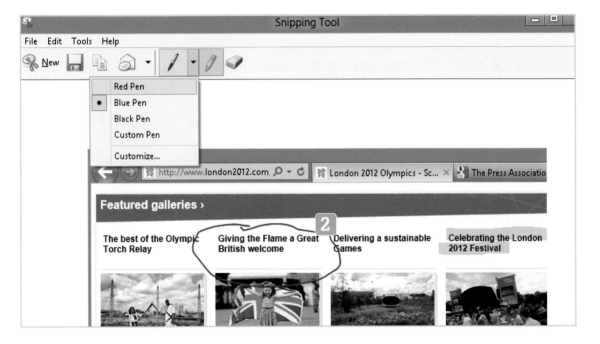

ALERT: If you select Email Recipient, this will insert the snip inside an email. Note that you can also send the snip as an attachment.

3 Click File, and click Send To.

4 Click Email Recipient.

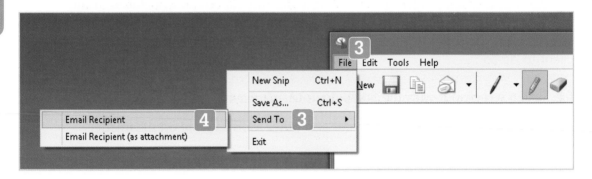

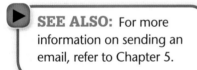
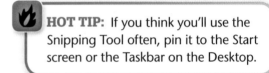

5 Insert the recipients' names, change the subject if desired, type a message if you wish, and click Send.

SEE ALSO: For more information on sending an email, refer to Chapter 5.

HOT TIP: If you think you'll use the Snipping Tool often, pin it to the Start screen or the Taskbar on the Desktop.

Record a sound clip

Sometimes the spoken word is best. With the Sound Recorder, you can record a quick note to yourself or others instead of writing a letter or sending an email. Sound Recorder is a simple tool with only three options: Start Recording, Stop Recording and Resume Recording. To record, click Start Recording; to stop, click Stop Recording; to continue, click Resume Recording. You save your recording as a Windows Media Audio file, which will play by default in Windows Media Player.

1 From the Start screen, type Sound Recorder.

2 Select Sound Recorder in the results.

3 Click Start Recording, then Stop Recording. If prompted to save the file, click Cancel.

4 Click Resume Recording.

5 Click Stop Recording to complete the recording.

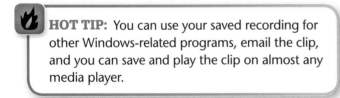

HOT TIP: You can use your saved recording for other Windows-related programs, email the clip, and you can save and play the clip on almost any media player.

6 In the File name dialogue box, type a name for your recording and click Save.

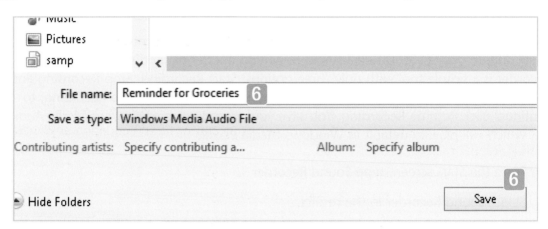

7 Click the X in the Sound Recorder to close it.

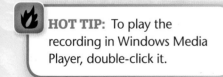 **HOT TIP:** To play the recording in Windows Media Player, double-click it.

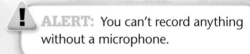 **ALERT:** You can't record anything without a microphone.

Explore other Desktop apps

There are many more Desktop apps available than those introduced here. All are available from the All apps screen, or you can simply start typing at the Start screen to locate them. Here are a few to try before moving on:

- Math Input Panel – write an equation with your finger, stylus or pen and this application will type it for you. You can then copy and paste the equation anywhere that accepts text.
- Paint – create flyers, signs, flowcharts and other artwork.
- Sticky Notes – create your own digital adhesive notes.
- WordPad – create more complex documents than is possible with Notepad.
- Windows Fax and Scan – create faxes and send them. You must connect a phone line to your computer to get started.

 HOT TIP: All Desktop apps open on the Desktop. You can't open Desktop apps on tablets that do not offer a Desktop feature.

 SEE ALSO: You'll learn about other Desktop apps such as Windows Defender, default programs and others in Chapters 13 and 14.

11 Work with files and folders

Introduction

You're going to have data to save. That data may come in the form of letters you type on the computer, pictures you take using your digital camera, music you copy from your own CD collection, movies you purchase from the Store, email addresses, videos from a DV camera and more. Each time you click the Save or Save As option under a file menu (which is what you do to save data to your PC most of the time), you'll be prompted to tell Windows 8 *where* you want to save the data. For the most part though, Windows 8 will *tell you* where it thinks you should save the data. Documents go in the My Documents folder, Music in the My Music folder, Pictures in the My Pictures folder and so on.

In this chapter you'll learn where files are saved by default and how to create your own folders and subfolders for organising the data already in them. You'll learn how to copy, move and delete files and folders, how to share data, and how to view data in different ways too. You'll also learn how to create a basic backup to an external hard drive, like a USB stick. All of this happens on the Desktop, and using File Explorer.

Explore your libraries

The four libraries (Documents, Music, Pictures and Videos) are available from File Explorer, a window that only opens on the Desktop. Each library offers access to the related personal and public folders. The first step in understanding how Windows 8 organises the data you keep and where to save data you create or acquire in the future is to understand these libraries.

1 Access the Desktop. (You can use the Windows key + D key combination.)

2 Click the folder icon on the Taskbar.

3 Position the cursor over Libraries, and if you do not see a down-facing arrow as shown here, click Libraries to show it (and the libraries underneath).

WHAT DOES THIS MEAN?

Library: A virtual storage area that makes it possible for you to access data that is stored in a personal folder (like My Documents) and the related public folder (like Public Documents), and any other folders or libraries you've created and/or specifically made available there.

4 Click the right-facing arrow by each library entry so that it becomes a down-facing arrow. Note the folders that appear underneath. Data is stored here.

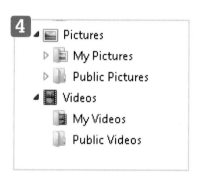

 HOT TIP: You will see more folders than the personal and public folders if they are available, if you have purposefully created or included them, or if they are available via shared folders on a network.

? DID YOU KNOW?

If you click a library in the Navigation pane, you'll see what's in both the personal and public folders. If you click only one of those, the data will be separated appropriately.

? DID YOU KNOW?

Your personal folder contains the following folders, which in turn contain data you've saved:

Contacts: This folder might contain information about the contacts you keep, such as email addresses, phone numbers, home and business addresses and more.

Desktop: This folder offers access to items on your desktop.

Downloads: This folder does not contain anything by default. It does offer a place to save items you download from the Internet, like drivers and third-party programs.

Favorites: This folder contains the items in Internet Explorer's Favorites list.

Links: This folder contains shortcuts to the Desktop and Recent Places, among others.

My Documents: This folder holds documents you save and subfolders you create.

My Music: This folder contains music you save.

My Pictures: This folder contains pictures you save.

My Videos: This folder contains videos you save.

Saved Games: This folder contains information about the games you play.

Searches: This folder contains information about searches you've performed.

Explore your personal folders

What is available under Libraries in File Explorer is not the only place you can save data; you have a personal User folder with additional options. To access these folders, you must know how to navigate there.

1 Open File Explorer.

2 In the Navigation pane, click Computer.

3 In the Content pane, double-click Local Disk, double-click Users, and double-click your user name. The 'path' appears in the File Explorer window.

4 Explore these additional personal folders.

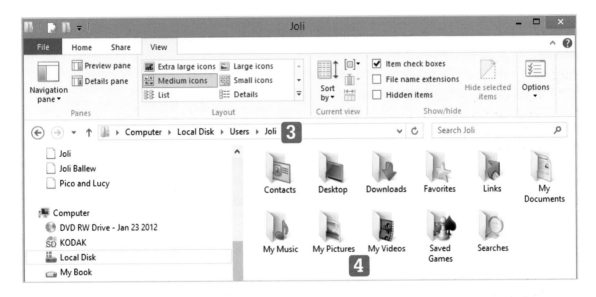

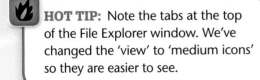
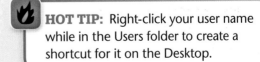

HOT TIP: Note the tabs at the top of the File Explorer window. We've changed the 'view' to 'medium icons' so they are easier to see.

HOT TIP: Right-click your user name while in the Users folder to create a shortcut for it on the Desktop.

Create a folder or subfolder

The default folders and subfolders will suit your needs for a while, but soon you'll need to create subfolders to manage your data and keep it organised. You could create subfolders inside My Pictures named Children, Pets, Holidays, and Friends, and then move related photos into them, for example. Likewise, you could create subfolders inside My Documents named Taxes, Health, CVs, and Letters.

1 On the Desktop, from the Taskbar, open File Explorer.

2 In the Navigation pane, select the folder to hold the new folder you'll create. (We've chosen My Videos.)

3 From the Home tab, click New folder.

? DID YOU KNOW?

You can right-click the Desktop or inside any folder, point to New and then click Folder to create a subfolder.

4 Name the folder and press Enter on the keyboard.

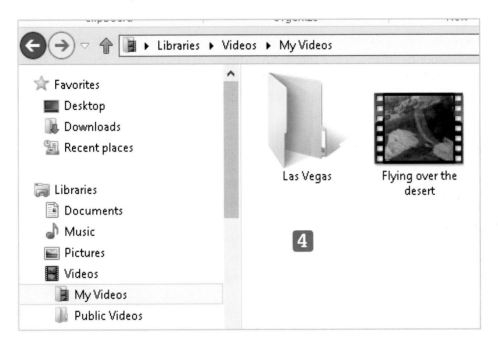

Las Vegas

Flying over the desert

4

! **ALERT:** If you can't type a name for the folder or to rename it, click the folder and from the Home tab, click Rename.

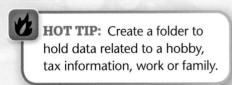 **HOT TIP:** Create a folder to hold data related to a hobby, tax information, work or family.

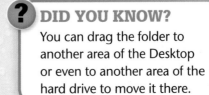 **DID YOU KNOW?** You can drag the folder to another area of the Desktop or even to another area of the hard drive to move it there.

Copy or move a file or folder

Folders contain files. Files can be documents, pictures, music, videos and more. Sometimes you'll need to copy a file to another location. Perhaps you want to copy files to an external drive, memory card or USB thumb drive for the purpose of backing them up. In other instances, moving is a better option, such as when you create a subfolder to organise data in a parent folder.

1 In File Explorer, locate a file to copy or move. Click it once to select it.

2 If the subfolder is available in the open folder, right-click the file and drag it there. Let go. You can then choose whether to move or copy the file.

3 If the subfolder is not readily available, click the file once to select it.

4 From the Home tab, click either Move to or Copy to.

5 Choose the desired location from the list. If you don't see it, click Choose location.

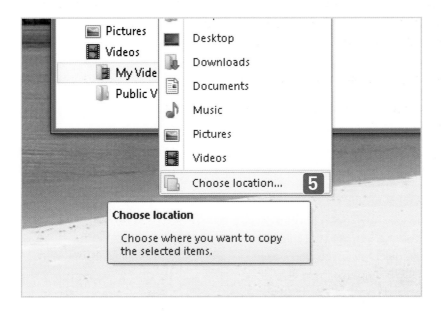

HOT TIP: Hold down the Ctrl key to select non-contiguous files or the Shift key to select contiguous ones.

Delete a file or folder

When you are sure you no longer need a particular file or folder, you can delete it. Deleting it sends the file or the entire folder (contents and all) to the Recycle Bin. This data can be 'restored' if you decide you need it later, provided you have not emptied the Recycle Bin since deleting it.

1 Locate a file or folder to delete.

2 Either:

   a Right-click the item and click Delete; or

   b. Click the file once and from the Home tab, click Delete.

? DID YOU KNOW?

It's best to keep unwanted or unnecessary data off your hard drive. That means you should delete data you don't need, including items in the Recycle Bin.

HOT TIP: Notice the other options available when you right-click a file or folder. You can copy, open, share, and more.

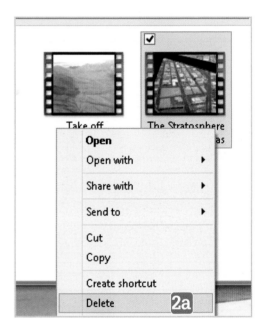

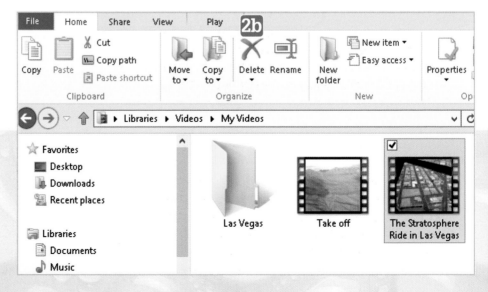

Search for a file

After you create data, like a Notepad document, you save it to your hard drive. When you're ready to use the file again, you have to locate and open it. There are several ways to locate a saved file. If you know the document is in the My Documents folder, you can open File Explorer and click Documents. Then you can double-click the file to open it. However, if you aren't sure where the file is, you can search for it from the Start screen.

1 Click the Windows key on the keyboard to return to the Start screen.

2 Start typing the name of the file or a unique word in the file.

3 Click Files in the Search pane.

4 Click the desired result.

> 🔥 **HOT TIP:** If you have to search for files often, it may be because your file system isn't organised very well. Consider spending some time creating subfolders and moving data into them to be better organised.

> ❓ **DID YOU KNOW?**
> You can search for a word *in a file*, such as a word in a document or presentation slide. You don't have to search using a word in the file name. The word will need to be unique though, so that the results don't offer too many files to browse through.

Browse for a file

On occasion, you'll be prompted to browse for (or locate) a file. You may be in a Start screen app, a Desktop app or you may be using a third-party online upload tool. The interfaces you'll see in each of these instances differ. To find the file you need then, you must have a good understanding of how the libraries and default folders are laid out. We think you do!

1 In any Start screen app, if you see the file to open in the resulting window after opting to browse, simply click it. You may then have to click Open, Upload, Select, or something similar.

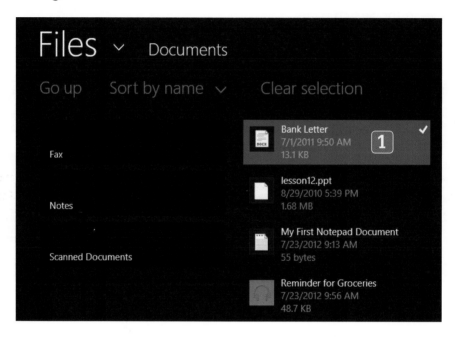

** HOT TIP:** If you always save pictures to the Pictures library, documents to the Documents library, and so on, you'll never have trouble finding your files.

2 In any Desktop app, if you see the file to open in any File Explorer window, double-click it.

3 In any Start screen app, if you don't see the file in the first list, click the down arrow beside Files and select the appropriate 'parent' folder, such as Documents, Pictures, Music and so on. Locate the file there.

4 In any Desktop app, if you don't see the file in the resulting window, select the appropriate parent folder from the Navigation pane. Locate the file there. Here we've navigated to a folder on a networked computer named Windows 7.

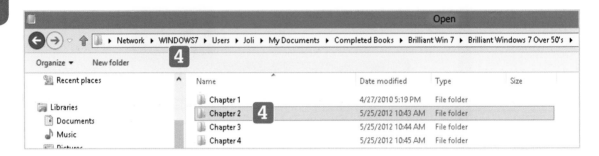

5 From a website, such as Facebook, click Browse and use the method required by the site.

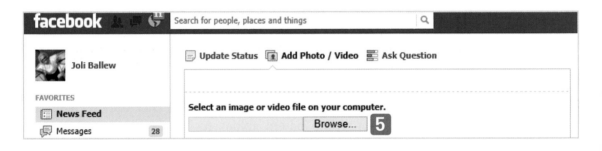

 **DID YOU KNOW?**
The path to the selected file appears at the top of the Open window when searching from a Desktop app.

DID YOU KNOW?
If you save your personal data in the available libraries, any backup program will include them in the backups it creates.

Change the size of an open window

A window can be minimised (on the Taskbar), maximised (to fill the entire Desktop) or be in restore mode (not maximised or minimised, but showing on the Desktop). When in restore mode, you can drag from any corner or edge to resize it.

1 A maximised window is as large as it can be and takes up the entire screen. You can maximise a window that is on the Desktop by clicking the square in the top right corner. If the icon shows two squares, it's already maximised.

2 When a window is in restore mode, you can resize the window by dragging from any corner or edge. An icon is in restore mode if there is a single square in the top right corner. You can access this mode from the maximised position by dragging from the title bar downwards.

3 When a window is minimised, it does not appear on the screen, and instead is relegated to the Taskbar. You cannot resize the window while on the Taskbar.

? DID YOU KNOW?
Hold down the Alt key and press the Tab key repeatedly to move through open windows on the Desktop. When you stop, the selected window will become the active window.

HOT TIP: To bring any window to the front of the others, click its title bar. This makes it the active window.

HOT TIP: You can quickly maximise a window by dragging its title bar upwards.

Use Snap, Peek and Shake

When working on the Desktop with multiple open windows, sometimes minimising, maximising and restoring or resizing isn't exactly what you want to do. Perhaps you want to make two windows share the screen equally; see what is behind the open windows, perhaps to see information on the Desktop; or minimise all of the open windows except one quickly. You can do this with Snap, Peek and Shake.

- Snap – to position two open windows so that each takes up half of the screen, using their titles bars, drag one quickly to the left and the other quickly to the right. Each will 'snap' into place.
- Peek – to view what's on the Desktop, position your mouse in the bottom right corner of the Desktop. The windows will become transparent and you can see behind them.
- Shake – to minimise all but one window, click, hold, and quickly move your mouse left and right on the window to keep. This 'shaking' motion will make the other windows fall to the Taskbar.

? DID YOU KNOW?
You can't do any of these things with Start screen apps.

HOT TIP: Close Desktop apps when you aren't using them. They will use resources in the background and could theoretically hamper performance.

Set Folder Options for all windows

There are already specific options applied to the folders you open in File Explorer. For instance, you double-click to open an item, new folders open in the same window (not a new one) and, if you have a touch screen, a tick mark appears on an icon when you select it. You can change these features and others from the Folder Options window.

1 Open File Explorer and click Libraries in the Navigation pane.

2 Click the View tab and note the layout. Here, that's Tiles.

3 Click Options, and click Change folder and search options.

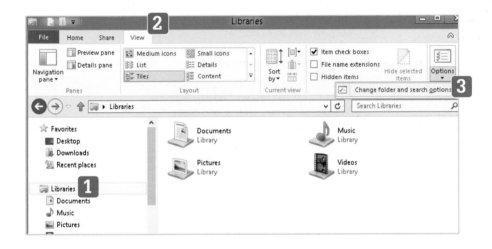

4 Explore each tab, making changes as desired.

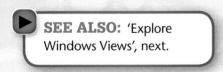

SEE ALSO: 'Explore Windows Views', next.

5 From the View tab, click Apply to Folders if you want to apply the changes to all of the other folders.

6 Click OK.

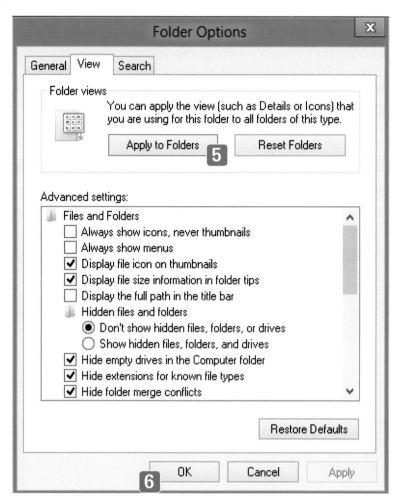

Folder Options

General | View | Search

Folder views

You can apply the view (such as Details or Icons) that you are using for this folder to all folders of this type.

Apply to Folders   **5**   Reset Folders

Advanced settings:

Files and Folders
- ☐ Always show icons, never thumbnails
- ☐ Always show menus
- ☑ Display file icon on thumbnails
- ☑ Display file size information in folder tips
- ☐ Display the full path in the title bar
- Hidden files and folders
  - ⦿ Don't show hidden files, folders, or drives
  - ○ Show hidden files, folders, and drives
- ☑ Hide empty drives in the Computer folder
- ☑ Hide extensions for known file types
- ☑ Hide folder merge conflicts

Restore Defaults

6   OK   Cancel   Apply

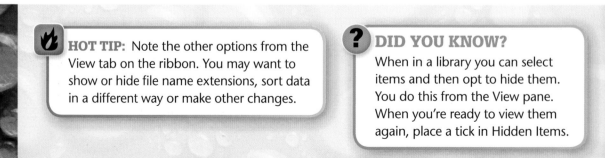

🔥 HOT TIP: Note the other options from the View tab on the ribbon. You may want to show or hide file name extensions, sort data in a different way or make other changes.

❓ DID YOU KNOW?
When in a library you can select items and then opt to hide them. You do this from the View pane. When you're ready to view them again, place a tick in Hidden Items.

Explore window Views

When you open most folders, you will see additional folders inside them. You'll use these subfolders to organise the data you create and save, such as documents, pictures and songs. You can change the appearance of the content inside these folders. You can configure each folder independently so that the data appears in a list, as small icons or as large icons, to name a few options.

1 Open File Explorer.

2 In the Navigation pane, click Pictures.

3 From the View tab, select a new layout. For Pictures, try Extra large icons.

UK 2007 VISIT - BATH +005   UK 2007 VISIT - BATH +006

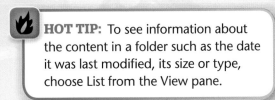 **HOT TIP:** To see information about the content in a folder such as the date it was last modified, its size or type, choose List from the View pane.

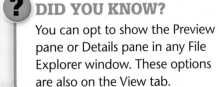 **DID YOU KNOW?**
You can opt to show the Preview pane or Details pane in any File Explorer window. These options are also on the View tab.

Share data using Public folders

If you want to share data with others on your network or with people who have user accounts on your computer, you can put the data in the related Public folder. It's often best, for instance, to put all of the music you own in the Public Music folder; you can then access that music from anywhere on your network.

1 Locate the folder that contains the data to move. (It may be on a networked computer.)

2 Select the data. You can hold down the Shift or Ctrl key while selecting to select multiple files or folders.

3 From the Home tab, click Move To, and then Choose Location.

4 Select the folder to move the data to.

5 Click Move.

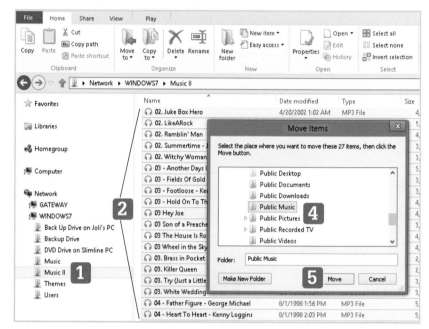

HOT TIP: Often, your new Windows 8 computer will have more hard drive space and a faster processor than any other (older) computer on your network. Thus, it may be best to move data you share to it, such as music, pictures and videos.

SEE ALSO: If you don't want to move data to Public folders, you can share your personal folders instead. Refer to Chapter 12 to learn how.

Back up data to an external disk

One way to back up your data is to copy it to an external drive. You can copy data to a DVD drive, a USB thumb drive, a network drive or a larger external backup drive (among others). You copy the folder to the external drive the same way you'd copy a folder to another area of your hard drive – you use the Copy command from the Home tab of any File Explorer window.

1 Using File Explorer, select the data to copy.

2 From the Home tab, click Copy to.

3 Click Choose Location.

4 Click Copy.

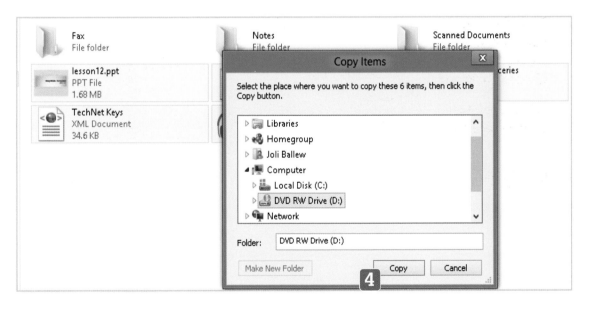

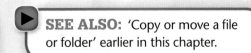

ALERT: Before you begin, plug in and/ or attach the external drive if applicable.

SEE ALSO: 'Copy or move a file or folder' earlier in this chapter.

12 Use public and private networks

Introduction

You've probably already connected to your own home network if you have one; this was part of the set-up process the first time you turned on your Windows 8 computer. You may not have optimised that network for sharing though. You'll learn how to do that here by setting up a HomeGroup, creating new users, and sharing printers, among other things. Beyond your own network, you can connect to other private networks (your parents' or one at work, for instance) as well as free, public wi-fi hotspots. The latter is especially useful if you own a laptop; you'll probably want to connect to other networks often.

Join a private network

You can connect to private networks at other people's homes and places of business. You can also connect to your own private network using this method if you haven't done so already.

1 Connect physically to a wired network using an Ethernet cable or, if you have wireless hardware installed in your laptop or tablet, get within range of your wireless network.

2 Use the keyboard shortcut Windows key + I to access the Settings charm, then click the Network icon shown here (it shows that networks are 'Available').

WHAT DOES THIS MEAN?

Private: This is a network you trust (like a network at a friend's house, at your house, or at work). This connection type lets your computer *diskover* other computers, printers and devices on the network, and they can diskover you. This is why you select Yes, turn on sharing and connect to devices. You want this to happen.

Public: This is a network that is not secure and that you cannot trust, like networks in coffee shops, airports and libraries. Choose No, don't turn on sharing or connect to devices, before connecting to these kinds of networks. You do not want to share anything here.

3 Click the desired network in the resulting list.

4 Place a tick in the Connect automatically box if you plan to connect to this network again, and then click Connect.

5 Type the required passcode, passphrase or other credentials as prompted. Click Next.

6 Click Yes, turn on sharing and connect to devices. This tells Windows 8 you trust this network and want to consider it a private network (vs. a public one).

? DID YOU KNOW?

Connecting to an existing network allows you to access shared features of the network. On a private network, this often includes data, media, printers and a connection to the Internet.

Connect to a free wireless hotspot

Wi-fi hotspots are popping up all over the country in cafés, parks, libraries and more. These hotspots let you connect to the Internet without having to be tethered to an Ethernet cable or tied down with a high monthly wireless bill. These are public networks.

1 Get within range of the public wireless network.

2 Use the keyboard shortcut Windows key + I to access the Settings charm, then click the Network icon shown earlier.

3 Click the desired network.

4 Place a tick in the Connect automatically box if you plan to connect to this network again, and then click Connect.

5 Click No, don't turn on sharing or connect to devices. This tells Windows you do not trust this network and want to consider it a public network (vs. a private one).

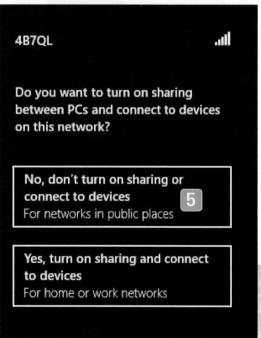

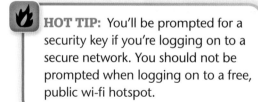
HOT TIP: You'll be prompted for a security key if you're logging on to a secure network. You should not be prompted when logging on to a free, public wi-fi hotspot.

ALERT: You'll need a laptop or tablet with the required wireless hardware to use a free wi-fi hotspot.

HOT TIP: To find a wi-fi hotspot close to you, go to http://maps.google.com and search for wi-fi hotspots.

Change the network type

If you made the wrong choice when deciding whether or not to turn on sharing and connect to devices the first time you connected to a network, you can change the setting. It's hidden away though, and is difficult to find if you don't know the trick.

1. From the Settings charm, click the Network icon.

2. Right-click the network you're connected to. If you don't see all of the options here, right-click a different entry for your network.

3. Choose Turn sharing on or off. Note the other options.

4. Select the proper setting:
   a. No, don't turn on sharing or connect to devices – for public networks.
   b. Yes, turn on sharing and connect to devices – for private networks.

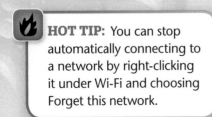

HOT TIP: You can stop automatically connecting to a network by right-clicking it under Wi-Fi and choosing Forget this network.

? DID YOU KNOW?

You can right-click a network connection and choose View connection properties to retype the passcode or change settings related to the network such as security and encryption type.

Set up a HomeGroup

You can share data in many ways using a variety of techniques. However, using a HomeGroup is the easiest. You create a HomeGroup in the Network and Sharing Center. Only computers that run Windows 7 or Windows 8 can join the HomeGroup, but you can still create a HomeGroup if you have a mixed network.

1 At the Desktop, right-click the Network icon on the Taskbar. Click Open Network and Sharing Center.

2 If a HomeGroup exists on the network already, you'll see Available to join. Otherwise, you'll see Ready to Create. Click the option you see.

3 Click Create a homegroup or Join now, as applicable.

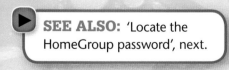

▶ **SEE ALSO:** 'Locate the HomeGroup password', next.

4 Proceed through the wizard by clicking Next and choosing what to share.

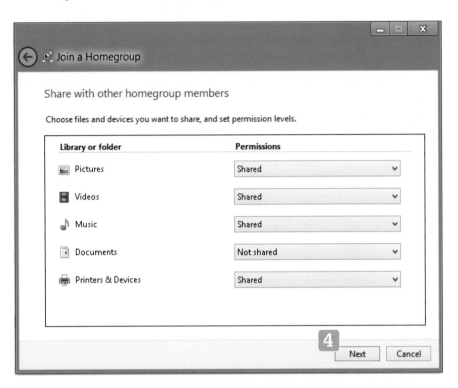

5 If you created a new HomeGroup, write down the password – you'll need it to allow other computers to join the HomeGroup. If you're joining an existing group, locate the password on another computer.

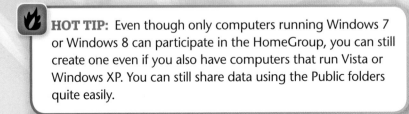

HOT TIP: Even though only computers running Windows 7 or Windows 8 can participate in the HomeGroup, you can still create one even if you also have computers that run Vista or Windows XP. You can still share data using the Public folders quite easily.

Locate the HomeGroup password

The HomeGroup password is available from the Network and Sharing Center, on both Windows 7 and Windows 8 computers. On either, right-click the network icon on the Desktop's Taskbar and select Open Network and Sharing Center to get started.

1 In the Network and Sharing Center, click Joined (beside HomeGroup).

2 Click View or print the homegroup password.

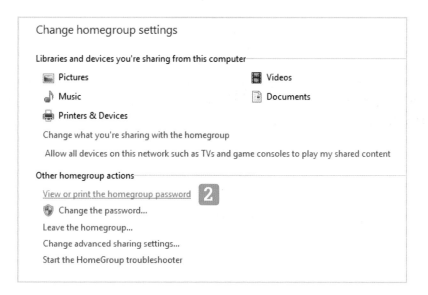

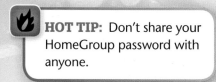

HOT TIP: Don't share your HomeGroup password with anyone.

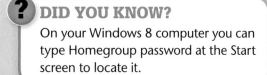

DID YOU KNOW?
On your Windows 8 computer you can type Homegroup password at the Start screen to locate it.

Create new users

You created your user account when you first turned on your new Windows 8 PC. Your user account is what defines your personal folders as well as your settings for Desktop background, screen saver and other items. If you share the computer with someone, they should have their own user account too. If every person who accesses your PC has their own standard user account and password, and if every person logs on using that account and then logs off the PC each time they've finished using it, you'll never have to worry about anyone accessing anyone else's personal data.

1 Click the Settings charm.

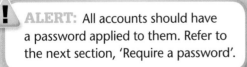

ALERT: All accounts should have a password applied to them. Refer to the next section, 'Require a password'.

2 Click Change PC settings.

3 If applicable, click Users in the left pane. Then, select Add a user in the right pane.

4 Work through the process to add a new user. It's the same process you worked through when you set up Windows 8.

219

> **? DID YOU KNOW?**
>
> The first account you created, probably your own, is an administrator account. Administrators have full access to the computer. Subsequent accounts you create are standard accounts. Standard users have limited access, permissions and rights on the computer for security reasons. You can change the account type in Control Panel.

Require a password

All user accounts should be password-protected. If you logged in with a Microsoft account, a password is already configured. If you use a local account though, you may have opted not to apply a password. Whatever the case, every account should have a password applied to it. This protects the PC from unauthorised access. To see if accounts exist that do not have passwords applied to them, view users in the Manage Accounts window.

1 From the Start screen type Users.

2 Click Settings, and from the results choose Make changes to accounts.

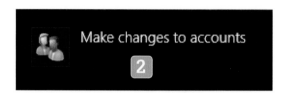

3 Verify each user account is password protected (and that the Guest account is off).

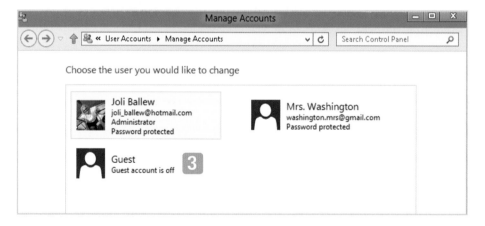

4 If you find there is a user without an account, take the necessary steps to enable one.

 **ALERT:** Make sure your password contains upper- and lower-case letters and a few numbers. Write down the password and keep it somewhere out of sight and safe.

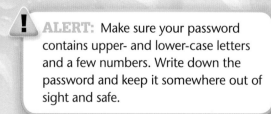 **DID YOU KNOW?**
When you need to make a system-wide change, you have to be logged on as an administrator or type an administrator's user name and password.

Use Public folders for sharing

You learned in Chapter 11 that you can share data with others on your network or those that share your PC, by putting data to share in the Public folders. The Public folders are located on your local disk, generally C:, under Users, and in the Public folder. In order to make sure that option is available every time you're ready to save a file, create a shortcut for it on the Desktop.

1 From the Desktop, open File Explorer.

2 Click Computer, double-click Local Disk, and double-click Users.

3 Right-click Public and click Send to.

4 Click Desktop (create shortcut).

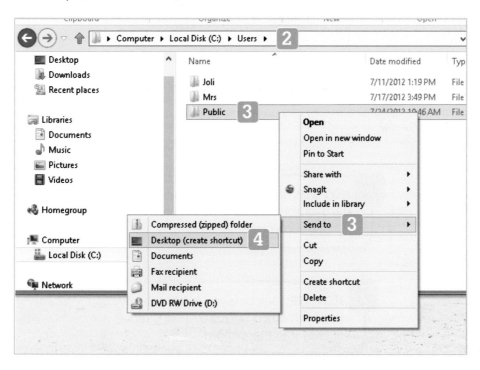

5 Close File Explorer.

6 The next time you save a file, either navigate to the Public folder in C:\Users\Public, or use the shortcut, shown here.

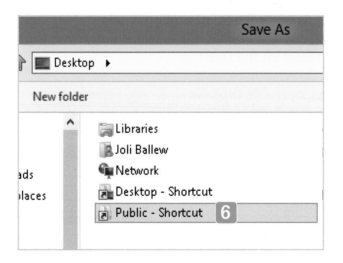

Save As

Desktop ▶

New folder

- Libraries
- Joli Ballew
- Network
- Desktop - Shortcut
- Public - Shortcut 6

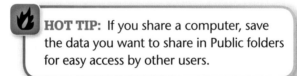

HOT TIP: If you share a computer, save the data you want to share in Public folders for easy access by other users.

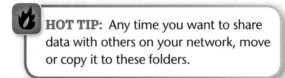

HOT TIP: Any time you want to share data with others on your network, move or copy it to these folders.

SEE ALSO: Chapter 11, specifically, 'Share data using Public folders'.

Share a personal folder

Sometimes you won't want to save, move or copy data into Public folders. Instead, you'll want to share data directly from a personal folder.

1 From File Explorer, locate the folder to share.

2 Right-click the folder, and click Share with.

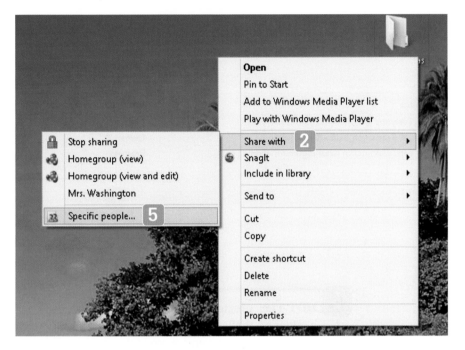

3 If you want to share with your HomeGroup or another user, select the appropriate option from the list.

4 Follow any prompts to complete the process.

5 If you want to share with specific people who are not in a HomeGroup, choose Specific people, then click the arrow and choose with whom to share. (Everyone is an option.)

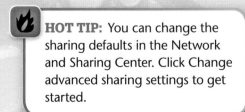

HOT TIP: You can change the sharing defaults in the Network and Sharing Center. Click Change advanced sharing settings to get started.

6 Click Add.

7 Click the arrow to set the permissions for the user.

8 Click Share.

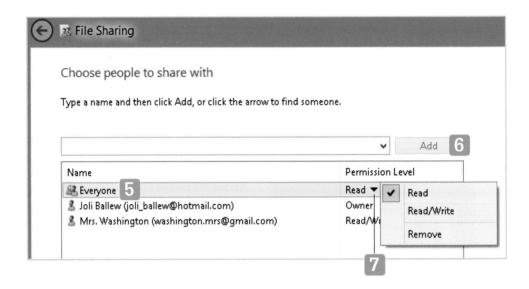

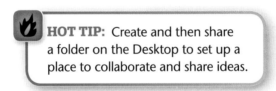

HOT TIP: Create and then share a folder on the Desktop to set up a place to collaborate and share ideas.

Share a printer

If you have a printer connected to your computer, you can share it. Likewise, you can access shared printers connected to other computers.

1 At the Start screen, type Printers. Click Settings.

2 In the results, click Share printers.

3 Verify Printers and devices is set to Shared.

4 To add a printer, repeat steps 1 and 2. This time, click Add printer.

5 Select the printer from the list.

6 The printer will appear under Devices.

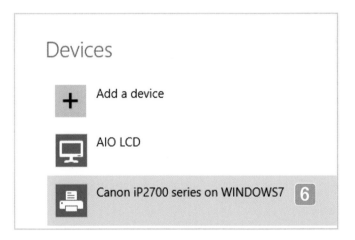

HOT TIP: To manually share a printer, open Control Panel and navigate to Devices and Printers. Right-click the printer to share and then choose Printer Properties. From the Sharing tab, select Share this printer.

ALERT: When others on your network access the printer for the first time, they may be prompted to install a driver for it. This is OK and will be managed by the PC.

Diagnose connection problems

If you are having trouble connecting to the Internet through a public or private network, you can diagnose Internet problems using the Network and Sharing Center.

1 At the Desktop, right-click the Network icon on the Taskbar.

2 Click Troubleshoot problems.

3 Work through the troubleshooter to resolve the problem.

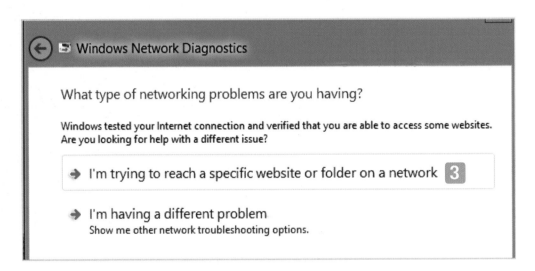

? **DID YOU KNOW?**

There are additional troubleshooting tips in the Help and Support pages. From the Start screen, type Help and Support. Then select Help and Support from the results.

! **ALERT:** If you are prompted to restart your network, turn everything off first. Then start the modem that connects your network to the Internet, wait two minutes, then turn on the router. Wait another minute and then turn on each of the computers.

13 Secure Windows 8

Introduction

Windows 8 comes with a lot of built-in features to keep you and your data safe. The security tools and features help you avoid email scams, harmful websites and hackers, and also help to protect your data and your computer from unscrupulous co-workers or nosy family members. If you know how to take advantage of the available safeguards, you'll be protected in most cases. You just need to be aware of the dangers, heed security warnings when they are given (and resolve them) and use all of the available features in Windows 8 to protect yourself and your PC.

Install anti-virus software

Windows 8 does not come with anti-virus software. You have to obtain and install this yourself. It's extremely important you do this if you haven't already; it will protect your computer from known threats, viruses, malware, and so on.

- You can purchase popular anti-virus software from well-known companies such as Kaspersky, Symantec, AVG and McAfee.
- You can obtain free and reliable anti-virus software from Microsoft Security Essentials. Visit www.microsoft.com to learn more.

- Once you've installed the software, configure the software to check for updates and install them daily.

 HOT TIP: Consider purchasing a book to help you learn more about staying safe, such as *Staying Safe Online in Simple Steps* by Joli Ballew, from Pearson Education.

 DID YOU KNOW?
If a threat does get by your anti-virus software, theoretically it can do less damage if you're logged on with a standard user account than if you are logged on with an administrator account. Consider creating a standard user account for yourself if you access websites often that aren't 'mainstream', where these threats are more prolific.

Verify security settings in Internet Explorer

Although you can configure a few security settings in the IE app available from the Start screen, the full set of settings is only available from the Internet Explorer Desktop app, available from the Desktop.

1 From the Desktop, open Internet Explorer.

2 Click the Tools icon and click Internet options.

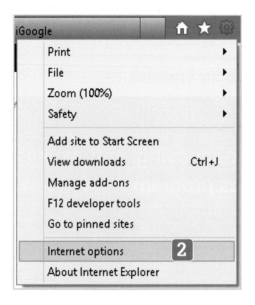

3 From the General tab, note you can delete your browsing history.

4 From the Security tab, note you can configure security zones. Medium-high is best.

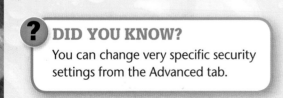

? DID YOU KNOW?
You can change very specific security settings from the Advanced tab.

5 From the Privacy tab, note you can turn on the Pop-up Blocker.

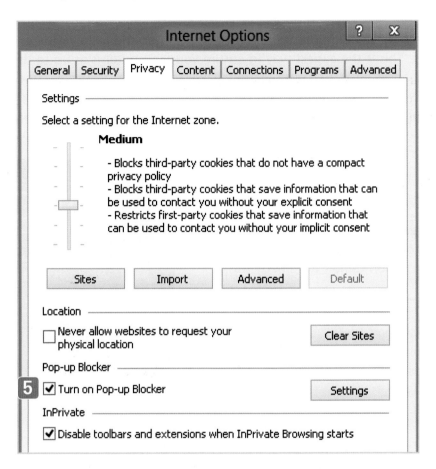

6 If desired, make changes and click OK.

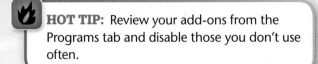

HOT TIP: Review your add-ons from the Programs tab and disable those you don't use often.

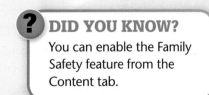

DID YOU KNOW?

You can enable the Family Safety feature from the Content tab.

Configure Windows Update

It's very important to configure Windows Update to get and install updates automatically. This is the easiest way to ensure your computer is as up to date as possible, at least as far as patching security flaws Microsoft uncovers is concerned, plus having access to the latest features and obtaining updates to the operating system itself. We propose you verify that the recommended settings are enabled as detailed here and occasionally check for optional updates manually from Control Panel.

1 From the Start screen, type Update.

2 Click Settings; click Windows Update.

3 Verify that your computer is set to automatically install updates. If it is not, open the Action Center to remedy this.

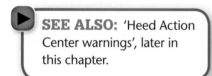
SEE ALSO: 'Heed Action Center warnings', later in this chapter.

Windows Update

You're set to automatically install updates 3

No important updates are available.   We last checked yesterday. We'll continue to check for newer updates daily.

Check for updates now

WHAT DOES THIS MEAN?
Windows Update: If enabled and configured properly, when you are online Windows 8 will check for security updates automatically and install them. You don't have to do anything and your PC is always updated with the latest security patches and features.

Use Windows Defender

You don't have to do much with Windows Defender except understand that it offers protection against some of the more common Internet threats. It is enabled by default and runs in the background. However, if you ever think your computer has been attacked by an Internet threat (adware, worm, malware, etc.) you can run a manual scan here. Windows Defender may be able to get rid of it.

1 Open Windows Defender. (You can search for it from the Start screen.)

2 Verify Windows Defender is enabled and note the option to run a scan if desired.

3 Click the X in the top right corner to close the Windows Defender window.

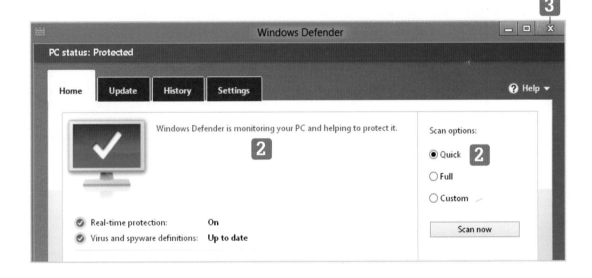

 HOT TIP: Click each tab available from Windows Defender to explore all of the options.

! **ALERT:** Windows Defender and Windows Firewall will probably be disabled if you've purchased and installed a third-party, anti-virus, anti-malware tool. Do not enable them if this is the case.

WHAT DOES THIS MEAN?
Malware: Stands for malicious software. Malware includes adware, worms, spyware, etc.

Enable the firewall

Windows Firewall is a software program that checks the data that comes in from the Internet (or a local network) and then decides whether it's good data or bad. If it deems the data harmless, it will allow it to come through the firewall; if not, it's blocked.

1 Open Windows Firewall. (Type Firewall at the Start screen and click Settings to find it.)

2 Verify the firewall is on. If not, select Turn Windows Firewall on or off, enable it, and click OK.

3 Review the other settings.

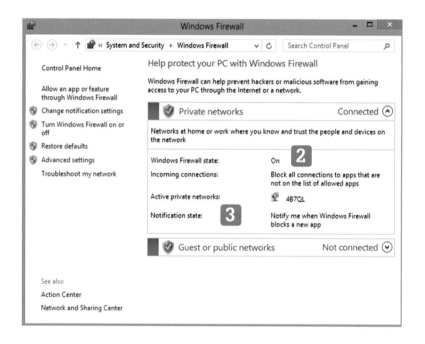

? DID YOU KNOW?
The first time you use a program that is blocked by Windows Firewall by default, you'll be prompted to 'unblock' the program. This is a safety feature to protect rogue programs from gaining unwanted access to your computer.

! ALERT: You have to have a firewall (either Windows Firewall or a third-party firewall) to keep hackers from getting access to your PC and to help prevent your computer from sending out malicious code if it is ever attacked by a virus or worm.

Heed Action Center warnings

Windows 8 tries hard to take care of your PC and your data. You'll be informed if your anti-virus software is out of date (or not installed), if you don't have the proper security settings configured or if Windows Update or the firewall is disabled. You can resolve these issues in the Action Center, a Desktop application.

1 From the Desktop, on the Taskbar, locate the Action Center flag.

2 Right-click the flag icon and then click Open Action Center.

! **ALERT:** When you see alerts, pay attention! You'll want to resolve them.

3 If there's anything in red, click the down arrow (if necessary) to see the problem.

4 Click the button that offers the resolution suggestion to view the resolution option.

5 If there's anything in yellow, click the down arrow to see the problem and solution.

6 Close the Action Center when all problems have been resolved.

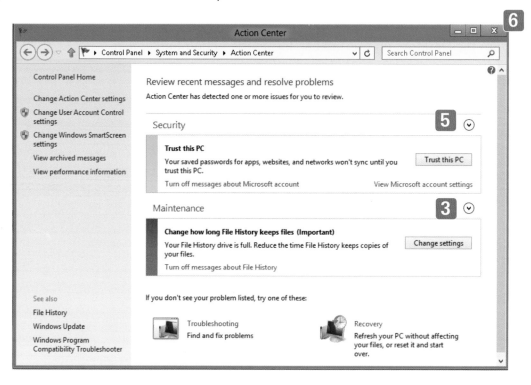

Use File History

Most of the security features in Windows 8 are enabled by default. File History is not. File History saves copies of your files so you can get them back if they're lost or damaged. You'll need an external drive for File History for it to be effective.

1 Connect an external drive or make sure a network drive is available.

2 From the Start screen, type File History.

3 Click Settings, and then click File History.

4 In the File History window, click Turn on.

5 Wait while File History copies your files for the first time.

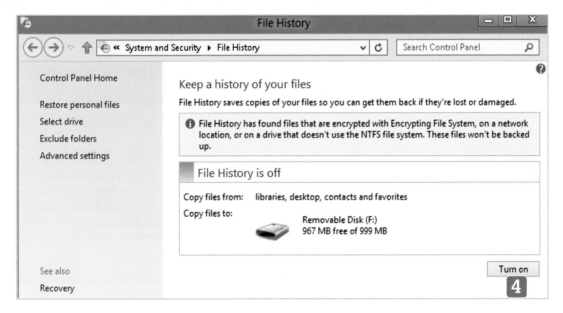

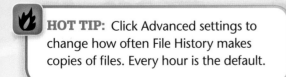 **HOT TIP:** Click Advanced settings to change how often File History makes copies of files. Every hour is the default.

ALERT: If you ever need to restore files using File History, open the File History window and click Restore personal files.

Verify User Accounts

You learned (in Chapter 12) that each user account on your computer should be protected with a password. You also learned how to verify that this is the case. Now you want to double-check this and remove unwanted user accounts.

1 Open Control Panel.

2 Click User Accounts and Family Safety, then click Remove user accounts.

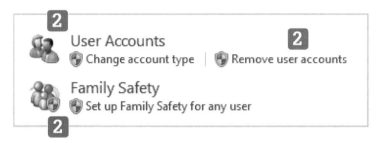

3 First, verify each user name has a password applied. Second, click any account to remove.

4 Click Delete the account.

5 Click Delete Files or Keep Files, as desired.

6 Do what is necessary to complete the process.

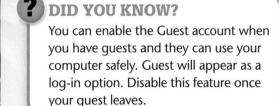 **DID YOU KNOW?**
You can enable the Guest account when you have guests and they can use your computer safely. Guest will appear as a log-in option. Disable this feature once your guest leaves.

 HOT TIP: If you have children set up as users on your computer, set up the Family Safety feature.

Configure a password protected screen saver

Your computer will automatically sleep after a specific amount of idle time (requiring you to input your password when you're ready to use the computer again), but you can configure a screen saver to engage after as little as one minute of inactivity. You can also configure your computer to display the log-on screen when you are ready to access the computer again.

1 Open Control Panel.

2 Click Appearance and Personalization.

3 Click Change screen saver.

 HOT TIP: If you regularly work on sensitive data that you don't want anyone else to see, make sure you set a screen saver to engage after a very short amount of idle time.

4 Select a screen saver, choose how long to wait, and place a tick in On resume, display logon screen.

5 Click OK.

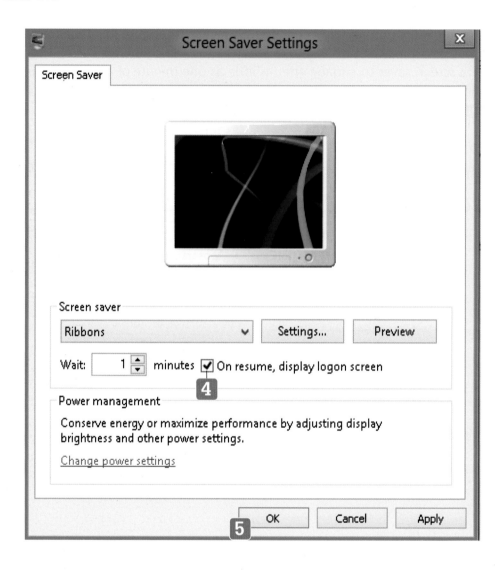

14 Fix problems

Introduction

When problems arise, you will want to resolve them quickly. Windows 8 offers plenty of help. If the boot-up process is slow, you can disable unwanted start-up items with the System Configuration tool. You can use Device Manager to 'roll back' a driver that didn't work or search for a new one. And if your computer seems bogged down, you can uninstall unwanted programs and apps easily to resolve whatever problems they are causing. You can even fix minor issues, such as the computer going to sleep sooner than you'd like or files opening in a different program than desired.

Change AutoPlay settings

When you connect a USB drive, a smartphone, a memory card, or insert a blank CD or DVD into the appropriate drive (among other things), Windows 8 asks you what you'd like to do. You can configure exactly what you want to happen in AutoPlay settings so that you aren't prompted every time, and so that the desired action happens by default.

1. Insert or connect media.

2. When you see the prompt, click it. (If you miss the prompt, diskonnect and reconnect the media.)

3. Click the desired action. The next time you insert this same media, the default action will occur automatically, and you will not be prompted.

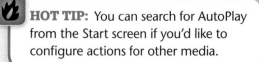

HOT TIP: You can search for AutoPlay from the Start screen if you'd like to configure actions for other media.

? DID YOU KNOW?
AutoPlay settings are located in Control Panel, under Hardware and Sound.

4 If you decide later to change the default action, open the AutoPlay settings. You can search for AutoPlay from the Start screen. It's under Settings.

5 From the AutoPlay window, you can change the default action you've already set or set new ones.

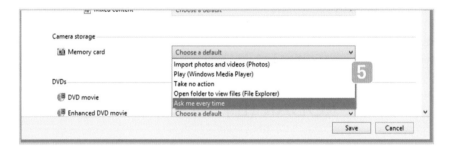

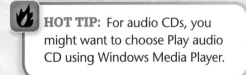

HOT TIP: For audio CDs, you might want to choose Play audio CD using Windows Media Player.

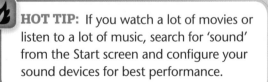

HOT TIP: If you watch a lot of movies or listen to a lot of music, search for 'sound' from the Start screen and configure your sound devices for best performance.

Change Power settings

Your computer is configured to go to sleep after a specific period of idle time. In addition, the display will turn off after a time. If you aren't happy with the current configuration, you can change this behaviour.

1 From the Start screen, type Power.

2 Click Settings, and click Power Options.

3 Next to the selected plan, click Change plan settings.

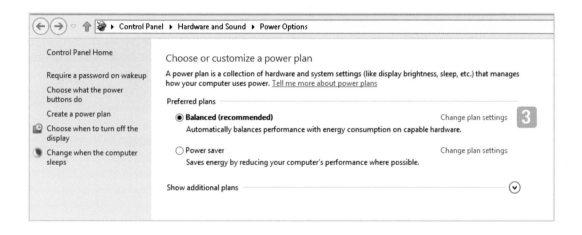

 HOT TIP: If you have a laptop or tablet, you'll see two sets of settings, one for when the computer is running on batteries and one for when it's plugged in.

4 Use the drop-down lists to make changes as desired.

5 Click Save changes.

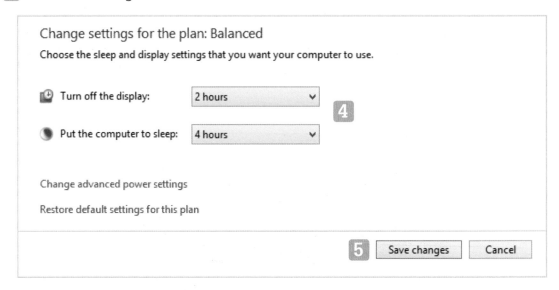

Change settings for the plan: Balanced

Choose the sleep and display settings that you want your computer to use.

🕐 Turn off the display: 2 hours ⌄   **4**

🌑 Put the computer to sleep: 4 hours ⌄

Change advanced power settings

Restore default settings for this plan

5   Save changes   Cancel

? **DID YOU KNOW?**

You can restore any power plan's defaults by clicking Restore default settings for this plan.

Fix driver problems

If hardware isn't working as it should be, you can search for a new driver. The driver is what facilitates the exchange of information between the device and the computer. If you download and install a new driver for a piece of hardware and it doesn't work properly, you can use Device Driver Rollback to return to the previously installed driver.

1 From the Start screen, type Device Manager.

2 Click Settings, and click Device Manager.

⚠ ALERT: If you see a red X or a yellow exclamation mark when you open Device Manager, that device isn't working properly or is working under limited capacity.

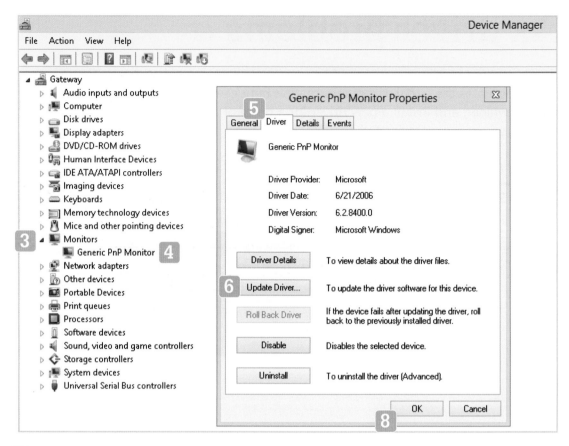

3 Click the right-facing arrow next to the problematic hardware (if applicable). It will change to a down-facing arrow.

4 Double-click the device name.

5 Click the Driver tab.

6 To search for a new driver, click Update Driver. To reinstall the previous driver, click Roll Back Driver.

7 Follow the prompts to complete the selected task.

8 Click OK.

? DID YOU KNOW?
The Roll Back Driver option will be available only if a new driver has been installed.

⚠ ALERT: You can rollback only to the previous driver. This means that if you have a driver (D) and then install a new driver (D1) and it doesn't work, and then you install another driver (D2) and it doesn't work, using Device Driver Rollback will revert to D1, not the driver (D) before it.

Use Disk Cleanup

Disk Cleanup is a maintenance tool that can help rid your computer of unnecessary files. This should improve performance and keep your computer running in tip-top shape.

1. From the Start screen, type Disk Clean.

2. Click Settings and then click Free up disk space by deleting unnecessary files.

3. If applicable, select the appropriate drive. Then, choose what files to delete.

4. Click OK.

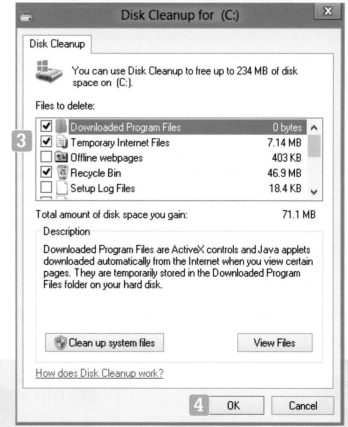

? DID YOU KNOW?

It's OK to select all of the options listed in Disk Cleanup and delete them all. However, you may want to keep items in the Recycle Bin until you're sure you don't need them.

HOT TIP: Run Disk Cleanup monthly.

Uninstall troublesome apps

It's unlikely that apps will be troublesome; they simply may not work as well as you'd like. You may also decide you don't need or want them. You can uninstall apps you no longer want from the Start screen.

1 From the Start screen, right-click the app to uninstall. (You can also tap and drag downwards to make the selection.)

2 From the toolbar, click Uninstall.

3 Click Uninstall again when prompted.

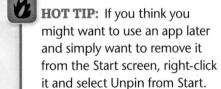 **HOT TIP:** If you think you might want to use an app later and simply want to remove it from the Start screen, right-click it and select Unpin from Start.

? **DID YOU KNOW?**
If you uninstall an app and decide you want it back, you can probably get it from the Store.

Uninstall problematic programs

If you haven't used a Desktop application in more than a year, you probably never will. You can uninstall unwanted or problematic programs from the Control Panel.

1 Open Control Panel.

2 In Control Panel, click Uninstall a program.

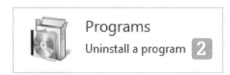

Programs
Uninstall a program **2**

3 Scroll through the list. Click the program to uninstall.

4 Click Uninstall.

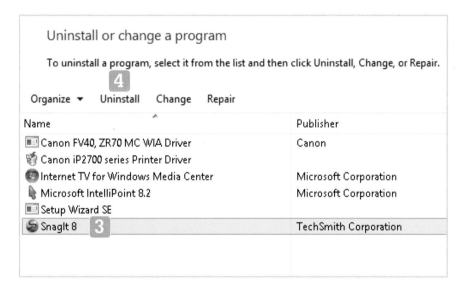

Uninstall or change a program

To uninstall a program, select it from the list and then click Uninstall, Change, or Repair.

4

Organize ▼   Uninstall   Change   Repair

Name	Publisher
Canon FV40, ZR70 MC WIA Driver	Canon
Canon iP2700 series Printer Driver	
Internet TV for Windows Media Center	Microsoft Corporation
Microsoft IntelliPoint 8.2	Microsoft Corporation
Setup Wizard SE	
SnagIt 8 **3**	TechSmith Corporation

5 Follow the prompts to uninstall the program.

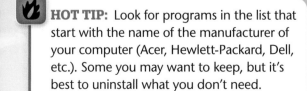

HOT TIP: Look for programs in the list that start with the name of the manufacturer of your computer (Acer, Hewlett-Packard, Dell, etc.). Some you may want to keep, but it's best to uninstall what you don't need.

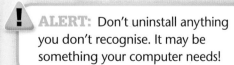

ALERT: Don't uninstall anything you don't recognise. It may be something your computer needs!

Disable unwanted start-up programs

Lots of programs and applications start when you turn on your computer. This can cause the start-up process to take longer than it should. Additionally, Desktop applications that start with Windows also run in the background, and can hamper computer performance. You should disable unwanted start-up items to improve all-round performance.

1 At the Start screen, type Task Manager. (You can also click Ctrl + Alt + Del.)

2 Click Task Manager in the results.

3 Click More details then click Startup tab.

4 Select a third-party program you recognise but do not use daily.

5 Click Disable.

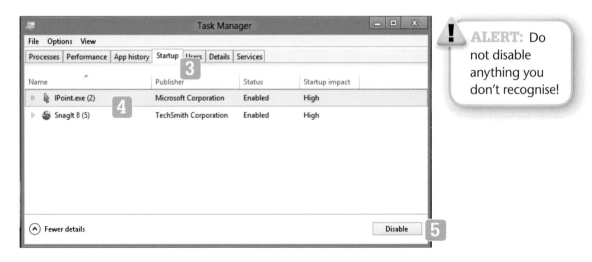

Apps   Results for "Task Manager"

Task Manager

2

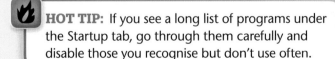

Name	Publisher	Status	Startup impact
▷ 🔋 IPoint.exe (2)	Microsoft Corporation	Enabled	High
▷ 🌀 SnagIt 8 (5)	TechSmith Corporation	Enabled	High

Task Manager

File   Options   View

Processes | Performance | App history | Startup | Users | Details | Services

3

4

⌃ Fewer details   Disable   5

ALERT: Do not disable anything you don't recognise!

? DID YOU KNOW? Even if you disable a program from starting when Windows does, you can start it manually when you need it.

🔥 HOT TIP: If you see a long list of programs under the Startup tab, go through them carefully and disable those you recognise but don't use often.

Refresh your PC

If your computer isn't running well, you can refresh it. When you do, all third-party programs you've installed from disks or websites are removed and your computer settings are returned to their defaults. This resolves almost all problems most users will encounter. Apps from the Windows Store will remain, as will your photos, music, videos and other personal files, so you won't have to start from scratch once the restore is complete.

1 Access the Settings charm.

2 Click Change PC Settings.

3 Click the General tab.

4 Scroll to locate Refresh your PC without affecting your files.

5 Click Get started.

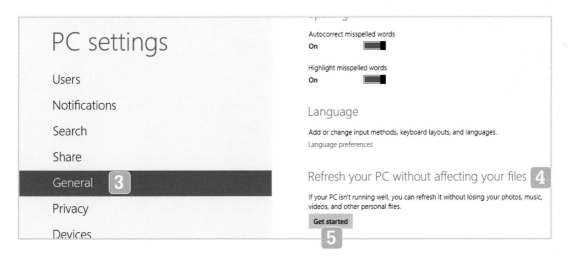

6 Read the information offered, click Next, and work through the refresh process.

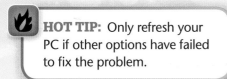

HOT TIP: Only refresh your PC if other options have failed to fix the problem.

ALERT: Before you refresh your PC, locate the product codes you'll need to reinstall third-party programs.

Reset your PC and start again

If refreshing your PC doesn't resolve your existing problems, then you'll have to reset your PC and start again. When you do, everything will be deleted, including all of your personal files. You'll need to back up these files before continuing here. This is a drastic step, so be sure this is what you want to do before you do it!

1 Access the Settings charm.

2 Click Change PC Settings.

3 Click the General tab.

4 Scroll to locate Remove everything and reinstall Windows.

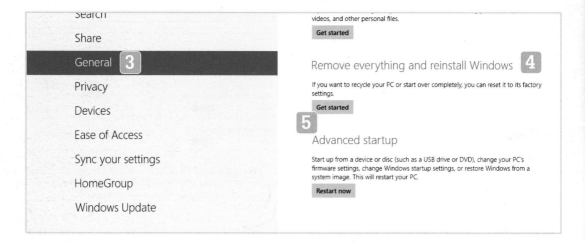

5 Click Get started.

! ALERT: Reset your PC before you sell it or give it away.

! ALERT: If you reset your PC, when it starts again it'll perform, act and look just like it did the day you brought it home!

HOT TIP: The option under Remove everything and reinstall Windows is Advanced startup. Choose this option to boot from a USB or DVD, change Windows Start settings, restore from a system image, and more.

Top 10 Windows 8 Problems Solved

Problem 1: I can't figure out how to shut down my computer

Your Windows 8 computer will go to sleep after a specific amount of idle time. When this actually happens depends on several factors including what power configuration you've selected and if the tablet or laptop is plugged in or running on batteries. The sleep state is quite efficient and doesn't use much energy, so it's often OK to let the computer go to sleep instead of turning it off each time you have finished using it. However, there will be times when you want to turn off the computer or tablet completely.

1 Access the charms and click or tap Settings.

2 Click or tap Power.

3 Click or tap Shut down.

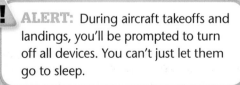
ALERT: During aircraft takeoffs and landings, you'll be prompted to turn off all devices. You can't just let them go to sleep.

HOT TIP: If you are relocating a desktop computer, turn it off before you unplug it.

Problem 2: I don't understand why I must use apps sometimes and Desktop apps at other times

An app is a simple program that enables you to do something quickly and easily, like check email, send a message, check the weather, or surf the Internet. *Apps* offer less functionality than their counterparts, the *Desktop apps*, but are easier to use and more streamlined. Here is the Internet Explorer app. You can't use apps on the Desktop.

Desktop apps are the traditional programs you may already be familiar with. Desktop apps are fully fledged programs like Paint, Notepad, Windows Media Player, Internet Explorer and similar third-party programs such as Adobe Reader. They open on the *Desktop*. They can't open anywhere else, such as in an app window. Here is the Internet Explorer Desktop app.

The Desktop is the traditional computing environment complete with Taskbar, Desktop background, shortcuts to programs, and so on. If you've ever used a computer you've used the Desktop.

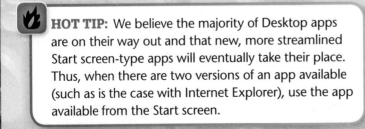 **HOT TIP:** We believe the majority of Desktop apps are on their way out and that new, more streamlined Start screen-type apps will eventually take their place. Thus, when there are two versions of an app available (such as is the case with Internet Explorer), use the app available from the Start screen.

Problem 3: The app tiles on the Start screen are flipping all the time and driving me crazy! Can I disable this?

Live tiles flip every second or two to show ever-changing information as it relates to the app. For example, the Photos tile will flip through pictures you've stored on your hard drive or on connected social networks, and the Sports tile will show the latest sports headlines obtained from the Internet. If you spend a lot of time at the Start screen, all of this flipping can become distracting. Alternatively, you may want to enable Live tiles for apps you use often, like Calendar, so you can keep up with your latest appointments without having to open the app itself.

1 At the Start screen, right-click the Photos tile. Note a tick mark appears by it. (On a touch screen, tap, hold and drag downwards.)

2 Note the option to turn the live tile off (shown here), or to turn it on (not shown).

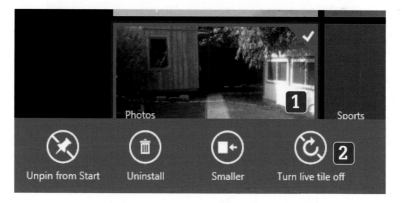

3 Click your choice, and then repeat with other tiles as desired.

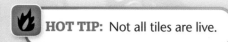 **HOT TIP:** Not all tiles are live.

HOT TIP: If you select a tile and then change your mind, just right-click it or drag it downwards according to your system.

? DID YOU KNOW?
If you want to remove a tile from the Start screen but you don't want to uninstall it from your computer, click Unpin from Start. You can always add it back later.

Problem 4: I can't get apps from the Windows Store

You need a Microsoft account. Here's why:

- You need a Microsoft account to use the Store. This is where you get more apps.
- You can upload, access and share your photos, documents and other files from places like SkyDrive.

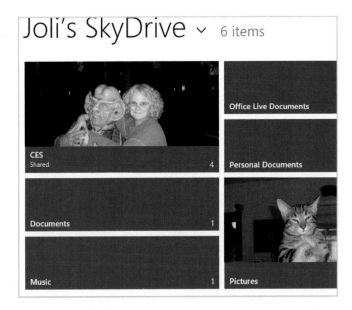

- You can log on to any Internet-connected Windows 8 computer (or tablet) with your Microsoft account. When you do, the personal settings you have already created on another Windows 8 computer are synced to it, including your themes, language preferences, browser favourites, browser history and apps.
- The apps you acquire in the Windows Store can be used on any Windows 8 PC you log in to with your Microsoft account.

 HOT TIP: You can sign up for a free Microsoft account at https://signup.live.com/. Alternatively, you can use your existing email address or obtain a new one.

 DID YOU KNOW?
You'll get a free personalised webpage when you sign up for a Microsoft account. There you can access your email, link other accounts, access Messenger and SkyDrive, and personalise the page with content, colours, themes and more.

Problem 5: I'm not getting all of my email in the Mail app. Why?

Just about all email accounts come with a 'junk' or 'spam' folder. If an email is suspected to be spam, it gets sent there. (Spam is another word for junk email.) Unfortunately, sometimes email that is actually legitimate email gets sent to this folder. Therefore, once a week or so you should look in this folder to see whether any email you want to keep is in there.

1 Click the junk or spam folder once.

2 Use the scroll bars if necessary to browse through the email in the folder.

3 If you see an email that is legitimate, click it once.

4 Right-click to access the charms, and click Move.

5 Click Inbox.

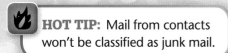

HOT TIP: Mail from contacts won't be classified as junk mail.

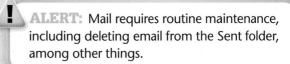

ALERT: Mail requires routine maintenance, including deleting email from the Sent folder, among other things.

Problem 6: My computer's display keeps turning off and the computer goes to sleep too soon

Your computer is configured to go to sleep after a specific period of idle time. In addition, the display will turn off after a time. If you aren't happy with the current configuration, you can change this behaviour.

1 From the Start screen, type Power.

2 Click Settings, and click Power Options.

3 Next to the selected plan, click Change plan settings.

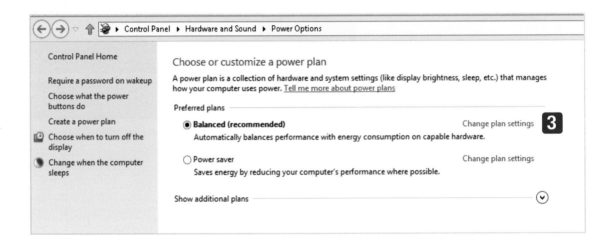

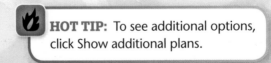

HOT TIP: To see additional options, click Show additional plans.

4 Use the drop-down lists to make changes as desired.

5 Click Save changes.

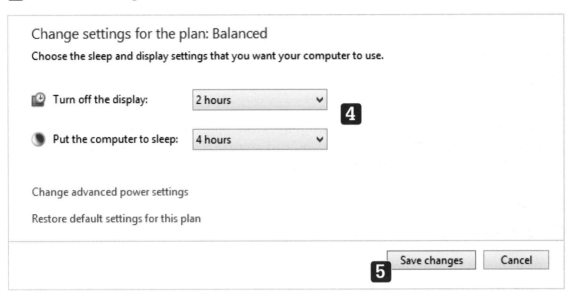

Change settings for the plan: Balanced

Choose the sleep and display settings that you want your computer to use.

Turn off the display: 2 hours   ∨   **4**

Put the computer to sleep: 4 hours   ∨

Change advanced power settings

Restore default settings for this plan

     Save changes   Cancel

5

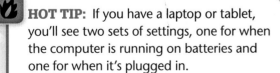

HOT TIP: If you have a laptop or tablet, you'll see two sets of settings, one for when the computer is running on batteries and one for when it's plugged in.

DID YOU KNOW?

You can restore any power plan's defaults by clicking Restore default settings for this plan.

Problem 7: I have an old software program I'd like to use, but it doesn't work in Windows 8

If you install a software program but it doesn't work properly, you can run it in Program Compatibility Mode. This lets you run programs made for previous versions of Windows. Often this resolves software problems.

1 From the Start screen, type Program Compatibility.

2 Click Settings.

3 Click Run programs made for previous versions of Windows.

4 Click Next to begin.

5 Choose the problematic program. Click Next.

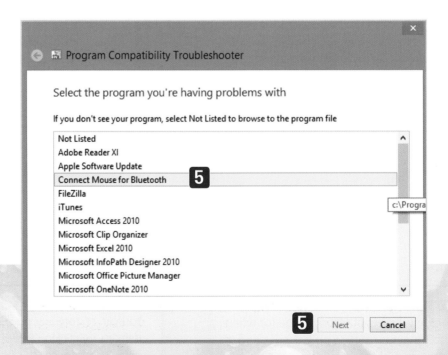

6 Click Troubleshoot problems.

7 Answer the questions as prompted.

⬅ 📄 **Program Compatibility Troubleshooter**

What problems do you notice?

7 ☑ The program worked in earlier versions of Windows but won't install or run now

☐ The program opens but doesn't display correctly

☐ The program requires additional permissions

☐ I don't see my problem listed

 HOT TIP: Don't run anti-virus software in Program Compatibility Mode.

 HOT TIP: Even programs made for Windows XP can be run in Program Compatibility Mode.

Problem 8: Where is all of my data? It's not on the Start screen

The four libraries (Documents, Music, Pictures and Videos) are available from File Explorer, a window that only opens on the Desktop. Each library offers access to the related personal and public folders. The first step in understanding how Windows 8 organises the data you keep and where to save data you create or acquire in the future is to understand these libraries.

1 Access the Desktop. (You can use the Windows key + D key combination.)

2 Click the folder icon on the Taskbar.

3 Position the cursor over Libraries, and if you do not see a down-facing arrow as shown here, click Libraries to show it (and the libraries underneath).

4 Click the right-facing arrow by each library entry so that it becomes a down-facing arrow. Note the folders that appear underneath. Data is stored here.

 DID YOU KNOW?
If you click a library in the Navigation pane, you'll see what's in both the personal and public folders; if you click only one of those, the data will be separated appropriately.

WHAT DOES THIS MEAN?
Library: A virtual storage area that makes it possible for you to access data that is stored in a personal folder (like My Documents) and the related public folder (like Public Documents), and any other folders or libraries you've created and/or specifically made available there.

Problem 9: Windows thinks my home network is a public network and not a private one. What can I do?

If you made the wrong choice when deciding whether or not to turn on sharing and connect to devices the first time you connected to a network, you can change the setting. It's hidden away though, and is difficult to find if you don't know the trick.

1 From the Settings charm, click the Network icon.

2 Under Connections, right-click the network you're connected to.

3 Choose Turn sharing on or off.

4 Select the proper setting:
  a. No, don't turn on sharing or connect to devices – for public networks.
  b. Yes, turn on sharing and connect to devices – for private networks.

 HOT TIP: You can stop automatically connecting to a network by right-clicking its listing under Wi-Fi and choosing Forget this network.

 DID YOU KNOW?
You can right-click a network connection (under Wi-Fi) and choose View connection properties to retype the passcode or change settings related to the network such as security and encryption type.

Problem 10: I can't connect to the Internet

If you are having trouble connecting to the Internet through a public or private network, you can diagnose Internet problems using the Network and Sharing Center.

1 At the Desktop, right-click the Network icon on the Taskbar.

2 Click Troubleshoot problems.

3 Work through the troubleshooter to resolve the problem.

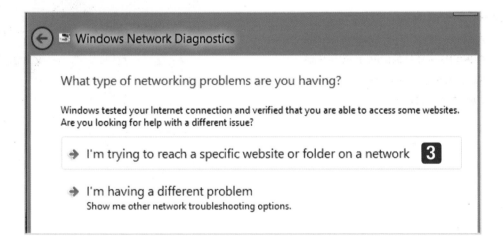

? DID YOU KNOW?

There are additional troubleshooting tips in the Help and Support pages. From the Start screen, type Help and Support. Then select Help and Support from the results.

! ALERT: If you are prompted to restart your network, turn everything off first. Then start the modem that connects your network to the Internet, wait two minutes, then turn on the router. Wait another minute and then turn on each of the computers.